HEAVEN'S
HEROES

HEAVEN'S HEROES

REAL LIFE STORIES FROM HISTORY'S GREATEST MISSIONARIES

DAVID SHIBLEY

New Leaf Press

New Leaf Press edition
First printing: June 1994
Fourth printing: March 2009

ISBN 13: 978-0-89221-255-2
Library of Congress Catalog Number: 93-87256

Unless otherwise indicated, Scripture quotations are from the New King James Version of the Bible.

Printed in the United States of America

Please visit our website for other great titles:
www.newleafpress.net

For information regarding author interviews,
please contact the publicity department at (870) 438-5288.

To heaven's heroes —
past, present, and future

Dear Young Reader,

This book was written for people like you, young men and women who want their lives to make a difference. The complaint of many young people today is, "I'm so bored." One thing we can promise you: If you give your life fully to Jesus Christ, you will never lack for adventure! Many of the people you will read about, and many people serving Christ around the world today, felt His call on their lives when they were about your age. It is important to hear what God may be saying to you now, not just when you're grown up. We hope God speaks to you as you read this book.

The Bible says, "One generation shall praise Your works to another, and shall declare Your mighty acts" (Ps. 145:4). The story of the worldwide advance of our Christian faith is the most thrilling saga in all history. Often it has been written in blood. We know your generation deserves to hear the awesome stories you are about to read. We know that our age group has a responsibility as parents and friends to pass these exciting accounts of courage to you. These stories are just too wonderful to die. And these people are too great to be forgotten.

We hope this book will be used in family devotions. The stories are great to be read aloud at family times around the table, in front of a cozy fire, or even in the car. We hope you will also read it alone, just God and you.

One of the hardest things we had to do was to decide whom to leave out! We made it a little easier by writing only about people who are already in heaven. That way we didn't have to choose among all the wonderful people serving Christ faithfully today. But there are also thousands of unsung heroes, people just as great or greater than the ones you will read about. Heaven has recorded each of their stories. One day we will hear them all.

We hope reading this book will whet your appetite to know even more about these real-life heroes. One book we have relied upon in particular is *From Jerusalem to Irian Jaya*, by Ruth Tucker, a history of exciting men and women in Christian missions.

As you read, you'll see we talk a lot about *world evangelization*. When we talk about world evangelization we just mean that we need to get on with the job of letting everyone everywhere know about, love, and serve Jesus.

We will be praying for you as you read. We hope you'll be praying, too. You're probably being pushed by somebody to take some kind of dare. Okay, we dare you, too. We dare you to pray, "Lord, make my life *count*," and see what happens!

We believe in you and what your life can mean for God's purpose on earth.

— David and Naomi Shibley

Forbid that we should ever consider the holding of a commission from the King of kings a sacrifice, so long as other men esteem the service of an earthly government as an honor. I am a missionary, heart and soul. God himself had an only Son, and He was a missionary and physician. A poor, poor imitation I am, or wish to be, but in this service I hope to live. In it I wish to die. I still prefer poverty and missions service to riches and ease. This is my choice.

— David Livingstone

CONTENTS

Opening Africa to the Gospel

Rowland Bingham

(1872–1942)

LET'S REMEMBER

> *And so I have made it my aim to preach the gospel, not where Christ was named, lest I should build on another man's foundation, but as it is written: To whom He was not announced, they shall see; And those who have not heard shall understand* (Rom. 15:20–21).

LET'S LISTEN

Rowland Bingham was heard to say, "I will open Africa to the gospel or die trying." He nearly died trying. But amidst the pain of friends' deaths and against seemingly insurmountable odds, Rowland succeeded in establishing the

Sudan Interior Mission and bringing the good news to the people of the Sudan.

Rowland Bingham had a happy childhood in Sussex, England. When he was 13 years old, however, life changed dramatically. Bingham's father died, and Rowland had to work full-time. He received Christ as his Savior through the Salvation Army and began his lifelong walk with the Lord.

While still a teenager, Rowland was drawn to opportunities offered in the New World. Not long after his move to Canada, God called him to preach. Soon he was an officer in the Salvation Army. But through contact with an elderly, praying woman named Mrs. Gowans, Bingham's life would be pointed toward Africa.

Mrs. Gowan's son Walter had studied special needs in the world. From this he decided the people of the Sudan in central Africa were some of the world's neediest. Sixty million people there had no Christian witness. Through talks and prayer with Walter's mother, Bingham became convinced that he should join Walter in attempting to reach the Sudan with the gospel.

In 1893, while in his early twenties, Bingham sailed with a college friend, Thomas Kent, to join Walter on his journey. Filled with excitement, they were stopped short when they arrived in Nigeria. "Young men, you will never see the Sudan," the head of a missions agency told them. "Your children will never see the Sudan; your grandchildren may." This disheartening warning seemed true, for Bingham soon became ill and had to remain in West Africa while the other two left on their 800-mile journey to the Sudan. Within a year, both were dead. Walter Gowans was captured by a tribal chieftain and, though he was later released, he died from a

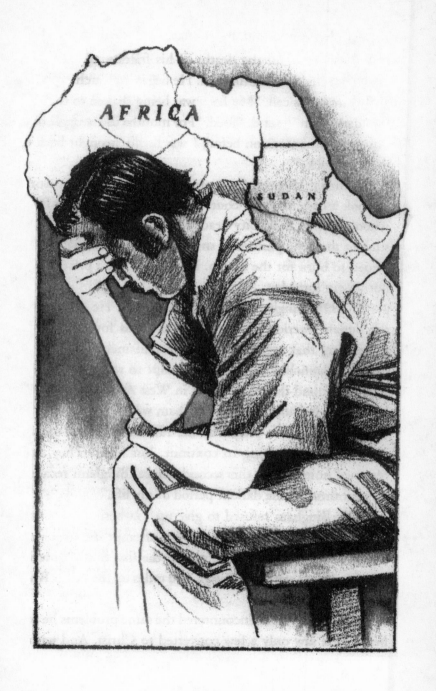

weakened physical condition. Thomas Kent died of the effects of malaria.

After hearing of the deaths of his friends, Bingham returned to England heartbroken. He began to search his heart to be sure of his call. "My faith was being shaken to the very foundation," he later declared. "For months the struggle over this great issue went on before I was finally brought back to the solid rock."[1]

Realizing his need for more training for missions work, he took a basic medical course and then enrolled in a Bible school in New York City headed by A.B. Simpson. While a student there, he pastored a small church, but his heart continued to burn for the Sudan. It was too dear a price to pay not to win someday.

In 1898, Bingham married Helen Blair. He also started the Sudan Interior Mission to raise funds for another try at opening that region to the Christian message. In 1900 Bingham launched his second attempt to reach the Sudan. Again he found the missionaries in West Africa had no sympathy with his hopes. Again Bingham was struck down with malaria and had to return home. His companions on this trip, though promising to continue, lost heart. They, too, returned home. After this second failure, Bingham recalled, "I went through the darkest period of my life."

Still, Bingham refused to give up. Gathering four more recruits in Canada, he made a third attempt the next year. This time he succeeded. He started the first Sudan Interior Mission (SIM) station at Patigi, 500 miles up the Niger River from the coast.

At first, Rowland encountered the same problems he had before. He saw only a few converted to Christ. And within four years, only one of his four helpers remained: one had died and two were sent home, too ill ever to return.

He did finally begin to see the fruit of his perseverance when he started new missionary stations that gave SIM a foothold in the region. A cure for malaria was found, which helped mission recruits live longer in the region. But more than anything else, Bingham and his assistants learned to pray with power. "There is the constant invisible warfare," Bingham wrote, "that has to be waged against the powers of darkness."

Over the years, the Sudan Interior Mission would start hundreds of churches. Missionaries established Bible schools for the training of Sudanese pastors. And the SIM built medical centers and became a primary force in the fight to rid Africa of the dreaded disease of leprosy.

When he was 69 years old, Bingham was amazed at the expansion of the gospel throughout the Sudan. Although the Christians were often tortured and even killed for their faith, the church continued to grow. Bingham had just completed a book about 50 years of life with the SIM in Africa when he died, apparently of a heart attack.

Nevertheless, Bingham had lived to see 10,000 people converted to Christ and nearly 1,000 churches began through SIM. It was one of the greatest success stories of Christian missions in African history, all because one man would not give up.

LET'S BE WORLD CHRISTIANS

Half of the world still has never heard the message of Jesus. Many of these people live in places that are hard to reach, just as the Sudan was for Rowland Bingham. These "hidden people" need to hear about Jesus. What will it take to get the message to them?

LET'S PRAY

Often the difference between having success or failure lies in the ability to keep on trying. Bingham's life challenges us to keep trying until we succeed. The Bible says "Though a righteous man falls seven times, he rises again" (Prov. 24:16; NIV). Ask God to give you the grace never to give up on a dream that He puts in your heart.

2

The Father of Modern Missions

William Carey

(1761–1834)

LET'S REMEMBER

> *I am a debtor both to Greeks and to barbarians, both to wise and to unwise. So, as much as is in me, I am ready to preach the gospel to you who are in Rome also. For I am not ashamed of the gospel of Christ, for it is the power of God to salvation for everyone who believes, for the Jew first and also for the Greek* (Rom. 1:14–16).

LET'S LISTEN

The man who would later be called "the father of modern missions" was born in a humble home outside of Northampton, England, in 1761. He had no unusual skills, no particular traits to indicate that he would shape the face of the church for centuries. Yet he did just that. In fact, he probably did as much as anyone else in history to stir the imagination of Christians for world missions. How was he able to accomplish so much? "I can plod," Carey said. "I can persevere in any definite pursuit. To this I owe everything."

Carey was converted to Christ and became active in church while still a teenager. He took a job as a shoemaker when he was 16 years old, and when he was 24, he began to preach in a small Baptist church in the village of Moulton and teach in the village school. During these early years of ministry, God was working into Carey's heart a deep desire to reach the unevangelized.

Carey married a childhood friend, Dorothy, and they had several sons. Their marriage, however, was not always a happy one. Dorothy suffered physical and emotional illnesses, though she and the boys followed Carey to India in his missionary undertakings.

In 1789, Carey accepted the pastorate of a large church in Leicester. His concern for those who had not heard the gospel grew, and in 1792 he published a small book that presented a powerful case for the church's involvement in missions. *An Enquiry Into the Obligation of Christians to Use Means for the Conversion of the Heathens* (this is the shortened title!) would eventually be ranked as one of the most important pieces of literature in Christian history. In the book, Carey wrote of Christ's Great Commission: "This commission was as extensive as possible, and laid (the disciples) under obligation to disperse themselves into every country of the habitable globe, and preach to all the inhabitants, without exception or limitation."

That same year, Carey preached a missions message to pastors in which he challenged them to "expect great things from God, attempt great things for God." In response to Carey's call, these ministers formed the Baptist Missionary Society.

Carey's zeal for world missions was not always appreciated. When he tried to encourage a group of Christians to reach the unreached, one man retorted, "Young man, sit down. When God pleases to convert the heathen, He will do it without your aid or mine." But Carey would not be silenced and his fire could not be put out.

Carey sailed for India in 1793. Arriving in Bengal, he immediately set out to learn the language. Although Carey was disappointed that only a few were converted to Christ in his early days in Bengal, he persevered in his study of the Sanskrit language and completed a translation of the Bible into Bengali. Then he set up a press to print the new Bibles. During this time he also established schools and began medical care for the people of the area. In 1800, Carey moved with his family to the Danish colony of Serampore. He would spend the next 34 years in that part of India.

Through the years, Carey would face many personal and family hardships. One of his greatest trials occurred in 1812 when his priceless manuscripts were destroyed in a fire. A massive dictionary of several languages, two grammar books, and whole versions of the Bible went up in smoke. But Carey accepted the tragedy as the Lord's discipline and began again.

Over the years, a list of what this one man accomplished is staggering. Along with his pastoral duties and preaching, he translated the Scriptures in whole or in part into 37 languages. He produced complete translations of the Bible into

Bengali, Sanskrit, and Marathi, and his stories in Bengali formed the basis for modern Bengali writing.

Carey founded the Serampore College for the training of Indian pastors and evangelists, as well as establishing churches. He founded the beautiful botanical gardens near Calcutta, for which he received the appreciation of all Asia. His influence also helped abolish *suttee*, the terrible practice of burning to death Hindu widows as part of the funeral service of their husbands, when the men's bodies were burned in a bonfire.

Carey died in 1834, but his impact is still felt across India and around the world.

LET'S BE WORLD CHRISTIANS

What great things are you expecting from God? What great things do you wish to attempt for God?

LET'S PRAY

How would you have reacted if years of your work were destroyed in a fire? Would you have the strength to start again? Ask God for the kind of strength that always gets you back up, even after bitter disappointments.

3

No Scar?

Amy Carmichael

(1867-1951)

LET'S REMEMBER

> *But Jesus said, "Let the little children come to Me, and do not forbid them; for of such is the kingdom of heaven"* (Matt. 19:14).

LET'S LISTEN

A young woman on the mission field in India, Amy Carmichael hiked alone to a cave in the mountain called Arima. "I had feelings of fear about the future. That was why I went there, to be alone with God. The devil kept on whispering, 'It's all right now, but what about afterwards? You are going to be very lonely.' And he painted pictures of loneliness — I can see them still. And I turned to my God in a kind of desperation and said, 'Lord, what can I do? How can I go on to the end?' And He said, 'None of them that trust in Me shall be desolate.' That word has been with me ever since. It has been fulfilled to me. It will be fulfilled to you."[1]

Amy Carmichael committed her life to serve the Lord as a single woman amidst the uncertain circumstances of life on the mission field. Her love for and faith in Christ would challenge Christians in their commitment and trust for years to come.

Along with several other missionary women in India, Amy established the Sisters of Common Life, a spiritual order of single missionaries committed to exhibiting "Calvary love." This love is still seen today in the ongoing work of the Dohnavur Fellowship, which cares for children throughout India. Amy's 35 books and numerous poems are a lasting legacy that have stirred missions involvement worldwide.

Born December 16,1867, in the village of Millisle on the north coast of Ireland, Amy was raised in a devout Christian home. Although Amy made a special commitment to trust the Lord in India, she witnessed God's protection and faithfulness years before she ever sailed for that country.

Amy's grandmother lived near the sea, where the tide is one of the strongest in the world. However, Amy and her brothers, Norman and Earnest, were permitted to go rowing within certain limits and were caught in a swift current.

"I was steering," Amy recalled. "My brothers were rowing hard, but they were powerless against the current. 'Sing!' they shouted to me, and I sang at the top of my voice the first thing that came into my head: 'He leadeth me, O blessed thought.' "

Strengthened by the words of the powerful hymn, the children were able to row the boat to safety.[2]

As a student in Ireland, Amy accepted the Lord Jesus as her Savior. Two years later, she had an experience that forever marked her values.

On a warm Sunday afternoon, Amy and her brothers were headed home from church. Suddenly, the three young people came upon a frail, elderly woman, bent over with a heavy bundle. Seeing her need, they offered to help the woman. Norman and Earnest lifted the load from the woman's arms, and Amy reached out to support her while she walked. Looking up, they noticed that several people from their church had stopped to stare. The scene was much like that in the story of the Good Samaritan, where the religious people passed by arrogantly while the Samaritan helped the robbed and beaten victim.

Later, when Amy remembered feeling the pain of the church people's self-righteous looks, she said, "I knew something had happened that changed life's values. Nothing could ever matter again but the things that were eternal."[3]

As a teenager, Amy went to care for Robert Wilson, the chairman of the famous Keswick Conventions (Bible conferences emphasizing a deeper relationship with God). Amy was drawn to these meetings because the teachings represented what she longed for in her life. Wilson's wife and daughter had died, so he loved Amy as his own daughter, and Amy cherished him, calling him the D.O.M. (Dear Old Man). When Amy was called to missionary service, the D.O.M.'s heart was torn, yet he knew he had to release Amy to God's will.

Her call to missionary service came clearly on January 13, 1892. Two words from the Lord, *Go ye*, were put deeply in her heart. Immediately, she made plans to serve the Lord

INDIA

~ HEAVEN'S HEROES ~

as a missionary. For a time she served in Japan; then she went to India where she served for 55 years without a furlough.

Early in her missionary career, Amy learned a hard lesson. She went to visit an old lady who was ill. As Amy spoke through her translator to this Japanese woman, she seemed eager to open her heart to the Lord. Then something happened. The old woman noticed Amy's fur gloves and became disinterested in the message. "I went home," Amy reflected, "took off my English clothes, put on my Japanese Kimono, and never again, I trust, risked so very much for the sake of so little."[4]

In Japan, Amy also learned to battle the powers of darkness. A Buddhist neighbor was possessed by the "fox spirit," as the Japanese termed it. Amy assured the wife of the demon-possessed man that she and other missionaries would pray until he was delivered. Within an hour, a messenger came to say that all the "foxes," six of them, were gone. The next day, the man, perfectly well, came to Amy with a bouquet of flowers to express his appreciation. Some time later, he died peacefully, with his New Testament in his hands.

Settling in southern India, Amy served first with the Zenana Missionary Society of the Church of England. There she was associated with Thomas Walker, the famous missionary to Tinnevelly.

In 1901, she formed the Dohnavur Fellowship with the purpose of rescuing children from the corruption of temple service. Often little girls were "married to the gods" during religious ceremonies and were forced to endure shameful abuse. Amy attempted to rescue these poor children and for years cried out against this social evil. Though the Indians knew this practice was one of the "secret sins" of Hinduism, many missionaries did not believe that such a horrible practice existed. Amy was often accused of kidnapping. The natives hated her, and the missionaries envied her. But she stayed at the task of rescuing these unfortunate children. By 1913, the Donavur Fellowship had housed and educated 130 children whose lives would have been a disaster without Amy.

Amy was also misunderstood for her insistence on "hearing the voice of the Lord" in matters pertaining to the Fellowship. Of course, Amy did not mean that she heard God's voice out loud. But she believed it was vital to hear Him on the inside and obey what was heard. She was able to "hear" God's voice because she stayed close to Him in prayer. Truly, Jesus was her dearest friend.

Amy left us the gift of her deeply spiritual writings — 35 books and poems. One poem asks if a person can possibly have traveled very far with Jesus without the scars of commitment:

No wound? No scar?
Yet, as the Master shall the servant be,
And pierced are the feet that follow Me;
But thine are whole: can he have followed far
Who had no wound nor scar?[5]

LET'S BE WORLD CHRISTIANS

Amy endured the pain of loneliness and being misunderstood in order to serve the Lord. What fears hinder you from being committed to serve Christ wherever you are?

LET'S PRAY

Pray that you too will be sensitive to hear God's voice in your heart.

No Greater Love

Jim Elliot

(1927–1956)

LET'S REMEMBER

Greater love has no one than this, than to lay down one's life for his friends (John 15:13).

LET'S LISTEN

"God, I pray Thee, light these idle sticks of my life and may I burn up for Thee. Consume my life, my God, for it is Thine. I seek not a long life but a full one, like you, Lord Jesus."[1] God answered this prayer of Jim Elliott. He burned with zeal to take the gospel to South American Indians, and he was killed when he reached them.

Jim Elliot committed to live for Christ at an early age. But it would have been difficult *not* to be a follower of Jesus Christ in the Elliot household. Living in Portland, Oregon,

Jim's parents were a godly couple who made sure their home was always warm and inviting for friends, especially missionaries.

In high school, Jim was outspoken in his commitment to the Lord. He took the Bible seriously and literally. And some of the conclusions he drew made him unpopular with his classmates. Nevertheless, most of the students respected him, and they elected him president of his senior class.

Jim's interests in high school led him to develop skills that would later help him on the mission field. From what he learned about architecture, he helped build simple churches in Ecuador's jungles. And his interest in speech gave him the ability to share his faith in Christ.

After high school, Jim enrolled at Wheaton College, a Christian school in Illinois with a strong commitment to missions. He liked the school's motto because it fits his own: "For Christ and His kingdom."

Jim gained a new appreciation for his home and parents during this first separation, which was reflected in this letter:

> This is the spring of my nineteenth year. Slowly I have come to realize that my arrival at this point is not of my own efforts, not merely by the sure ticking of this winged racer Time, but by the quiet, unfelt guidance of a faithful mother and a father-preacher who has not spent so much time rearing other people's children that he hasn't had time for his own. . . . I am grateful to you and to our mutual Father, who has loved us all with a Love unknowable.[2]

While at Wheaton, Jim collected his thoughts in a diary, which was published after his death as a book called *Jim Elliot's Journal*. This journal contains some of the most deeply spiritual ideas recorded in the 20th century. His life's message is perhaps best described in the words he wrote at Wheaton in 1949: "He is no fool who gives what he cannot keep to gain what he cannot lose."

While in college, Jim became even more interested in primitive peoples not yet reached with the gospel. He gained physical strength as a champion wrestler and majored in New Testament Greek so he would be better equipped as a Bible translator. The degree he most desired, however, was what he termed the A.U.G. degree — Approved unto God.

Jim knew that the kind of missions work he wanted to pursue was dangerous, for many of the tribes were truly savage. Yet Jim comforted himself in God's sovereign direction. He wrote his brother, encouraging him to boldly obey God's leading: "You are immortal until your work is finished."

Jim Elliot believed that the greatest qualification for effectiveness in Christian work was godly living. In his journal he wrote, "I see tonight that in spiritual work, if nowhere else, the character of the worker decides the quality of the work. . . . No wonder so much work in the Kingdom today is shoddy — look at the moral character of the worker."[3]

After graduation, he continued to prepare to be a missionary while awaiting approval from his local church. During this time, as God was focusing Jim's attention on the Quichuas, a vast Indian community in South America, he wrote, "Consider the call from the throne above, 'Go ye,' and from round about, 'come over and help us,' and even the call from the damned souls below, 'Send Lazarus to my brothers, that they come not to this place.' Impelled, then, by these voices, I dare not stay home while Quichuas perish."[4]

Finally, the day he had prayed for came. On February 4, 1952, Jim Elliot departed by ship with Pete Fleming for Ecuador. Jim's parents were on the pier, weeping with joy as their son's ship sailed out of sight.

Jim launched into his work with youthful vigor. After several happy months in Quito, the capital, Jim went farther into the interior of Ecuador, to Shandia, a village at the base of the magnificent Andes mountain range. Earlier, at Wheaton, Jim had met a fellow student named Elisabeth Howard, who shared his deep spirituality and attraction to missions. Through the years since college, Jim and Elisabeth had allowed God to rule their romance and now their faith was rewarded. They were married in a simple service in Quito on October 8, 1953. This happy young missionary couple worked well as a team, ministering to the Quichuas. Their only child, Valerie, was born in February of 1955.

More and more, Jim pursued tribes who had not yet heard the gospel. He knew that God had promised that there would be people from every tribe among the redeemed. Around the throne, the redeemed would one day sing, "You . . . have redeemed us to God by Your blood out of every tribe and tongue and people and nation" (Rev. 5:9). Elliot wrote, "This is specific indication that the gospel must be gotten to tribes who are not yet included in the singing hosts. Hence, my burden for cultural groups as yet untouched."[5] For Elliot, this burden pointed in a clear direction — toward the Aucas.

The Aucas were a feared, savage tribe, who seemed straight out of the Stone Age. These isolated manhunters had successfully fought off any intrusion of civilization. They numbered

in the thousands and were untouched by the good news of Jesus Christ. Few from the outside had ever entered Auca territory. Even fewer had come back.

Elliot and four other young missionaries decided it was their responsibility to reach the Aucas. "The prayer that had been in Jim's heart for years was prayed with renewed energy now — that those who still had never heard, who had never even had the chance to reject the gospel message, might hear. Many Quichuas had heard; many had rejected; but their blood was now upon their own hands. The blood of the Aucas, however, Jim saw on his own."[6]

Preliminary flights were made over Auca land. Gestures of friendship were made from the low-flying plane; gifts were dropped to the Aucas. Then it was time to go personally, to risk face to face encounters with the Aucas.

Before the trip, Jim and Elisabeth finished a translation of the Gospel of Luke for the Quichuas. They also talked frankly about the possibility that he might not return. Yet Jim believed the time was right.

The five brave missionaries penetrated Auca territory and made friendly contact with an Auca woman. Encouraged, the men radioed their wives to keep praying. But soon the transmissions went still, and communications ceased. On January 8, 1956, Jim Elliot and the four other missionaries were brutally murdered by those they had attempted to reach with God's message of love.

The true heroes of this story are not only the men who laid down their lives for Christ, but also the brave wives and families who picked up the pieces of their shattered hopes and continued to serve the Lord. Elisabeth Elliot, with their young daughter, determined that now, more than ever, the

Aucas must have the gospel. Along with the others, they lived among the Aucas, courageously forgiving the very men who had murdered their husband and father. Today, hundreds of Aucas are Christians. They are even sending some of their own people as missionaries to surrounding tribes.

When the news of the death of the five missionaries was announced in Christian schools, hundreds of young people volunteered to take their place. The story caused world mission to be front-page news in *Life* magazine and newspapers around the world. Elisabeth's books about Jim's death, *Through Gates of Splendor*, and his life, *Shadow of the Almighty*, became missionary classics. Thousands of people today are challenged by *The Journal of Jim Elliot*. ". . . He being dead still speaks" (Heb.11:4).

Today, Elisabeth continues her ministry of speaking and writing. Valerie is married to a pastor. The Aucas have been evangelized. And Jim Elliot, having surrendered what he could not keep, has gained what he could not lose.

LET'S BE WORLD CHRISTIANS

Jim Elliot was willing to risk his life to get the gospel to an unreached group of people. Was it too high a price to pay?

LET'S PRAY

Pray that God will enable you to live for what really matters, that you will be willing to give up what cannot be kept anyway to gain what can never be lost.

5

The Father of Modern Evangelism

Charles E. Fuller

(1887–1968)

LET'S REMEMBER

> *To the weak I became as weak, that I might win the weak. I have become all things to all men, that I might by all means save some. Now this I do for the gospel's sake, that I may be partaker of it with you* (1 Cor. 9:22–23).

LET'S LISTEN

Charles E. Fuller wanted to use every available means "to get the gospel out" to as many people as possible, and the newest way of sending the gospel in Fuller's day was by radio. So he started the "Old Fashioned Revival Hour" radio program. And, though he did not go overseas as a missionary,

Fuller's voice was heard around the world, bringing the message of Jesus.

The "Old Fashioned Revival Hour" drew larger audiences than any other program aired during radio's golden years of the 1940s. Twenty million people tuned in to the Sunday program, a larger audience than any Christian broadcast or telecast has today.

Charles Fuller was born in Los Angeles to devout Christian parents. His father, who had been converted under the preaching of D.L. Moody, led his four sons in daily devotions, directing them in their relationships with the Lord.

Young Fuller excelled in athletics and academics. Captain of his college football team, he graduated with honors and later used his degree in chemistry to help manage his father's orange groves.

After college Charles married his high school sweetheart, Grace Payton. "Honey," as he called her, later became the warm voice reading mail on the broadcast. In 1916, Charles Fuller attended a meeting conducted by evangelist Paul Rader because he wanted to hear what the former prizefighter had to say about Christianity. After the service, deeply moved by the Holy Spirit, Fuller drove his car to nearby Franklin Park in Hollywood. There he knelt on the floor of the back seat and gave his life to Christ. He later recalled:

> There had come a complete change into my life. Sunday, I went up to Los Angeles and heard Paul Rader preach. I never heard such a sermon in all my life. Ephesians 1:18. Now my whole life's aims and ambitions are changed. I feel now that I want to serve God if He can use me instead of making the

goal of my life the making of money. I may have a call to go to the mission field in Africa.[1]

Both he and Grace entered the Bible Institute of Los Angeles (now Biola University) to prepare for Christian service. The godly dean of the Institute, Dr. R.A. Torrey, told Fuller just before his graduation, "Young man, God has a great work for you."

Charles Fuller's popularity as a Bible teacher began to spread. He was ordained as a minister and pastored the Calvary Church in Placentia until 1933. Even in his early years of preaching, he stressed missions and evangelism.

Late one night, Charles Fuller awakened with thoughts of using radio to get the message of God's love to the people who might never go to church. At first, Fuller struggled with this call of God because he knew that it would be difficult to sustain a listening audience and maintain financial responsibility. His innovative use of radio to broadcast the good news was a bold step. He would later be called "the father of modern evangelism" because of his use of mass media to spread the gospel. Thus, he was the forerunner of a long stream of evangelists who later used television to bring God's message to the people.

However, Fuller obeyed God's directive and, throughout his life, he continued to try new ways to advance the message of Christ. He held large evangelistic rallies, helped sponsor 100 evangelists, founded a seminary with missions and evangelism as the heartthrob of the school, and carried on an international broadcast.

Before Billy Graham became a national evangelist, Charles Fuller conducted some of the largest evangelistic meetings in the country. Twice during his outdoor rallies, rain threatened to stop the meetings. On both occasions, the rain stopped immediately after Dr. Fuller prayed. In Chicago in 1946, with 68,000 people present, someone said the rain stopped as if someone "had turned off a faucet."

In the 1930s, during the Great Depression, times were hard for many American families. The Fullers, along with millions of others, had very little money. Their only son, Daniel, was seriously ill. Still, God gave the Fullers the promise from His Word that "great and mighty things" were in store for them.

Soon, the broadcast Fuller had begun was picked up by other radio stations. He seemed to be touching a heartstring in America's soul. Through the brutal years of the Depression in the 1930s and World War II in the 1940s, Charles Fuller and the "Old Fashioned Revival Hour" stood as a national symbol of hope and encouragement. During the war years, the Sunday afternoon service Fuller conducted from the Long Beach Municipal Auditorium was heard in many parts of the world. Ushers reserved 250 seats at the front of the auditorium for men and women in military service. Hundreds of young men who would later lose their lives in battle gave their hearts to Christ in those meetings. Fuller knew about this because he had asked Dawson Trotman, of the Navigators ministry, to help keep in touch with these new Christians.

In 1947, Charles expanded his international ministry by helping to found the Fuller Theological Seminary. Today the School of World Mission at Fuller Seminary trains Christian workers from many parts of the world.

Charles Fuller championed the little people, those in the "out-of-the-way places" — the shut-ins, the small farmers, the lonely soldiers. He reached them with the sincerity and compassion of his voice. His messages touched their hearts at their time of need.

Dr. Fuller's driving passion was to see people come to a saving knowledge of Jesus Christ: "My ambition is to see the world evangelized in this generation. I believe two things must be done before my responsibility has been fulfilled. First, to seek to be as effective as possible in preaching by radio; and second, to train others to preach."

On March 18, 1968, Charles Fuller went home to heaven. His life was, perhaps, best summarized by Harold Ockenga, his long-time friend and co-founder of Fuller Seminary: "Here was a man of faith who took great risks for God."

LET'S BE WORLD CHRISTIANS

In his time, Charles Fuller saw radio broadcasts as a new, exciting way to get God's news to more people. What are some new ways in our day to spread the gospel?

LET'S PRAY

Charles Fuller wanted the message of Christ to reach the "out-of-the-way places." Let's pray today for unreached peoples who have not yet heard of Christ and His love for them.

6

BEFORE WE KILL AND EAT YOU

H.B. GARLOCK

(1897–1985)

LET'S REMEMBER

> *And He said to them, "Go into all the world and preach the gospel to every creature"* (Mark 16:15).

LET'S LISTEN

H.B. Garlock was one of the last of the great wave of missionary pioneers to western Africa. Even though he lived in the 20th century, many of his missions adventures read like those of Paul in the Book of Acts.

The eldest of 12 children, Garlock was raised by God-fearing parents. He began to serve the Lord when he was a child, but at age 16, Christmas Day 1913, he had a powerful encounter with the Holy Spirit. Soon he determined to leave the family farm in Connecticut to go to Bible school.

His life was almost cut short by the influenza epidemic that swept the country immediately after World War I. While he was very ill, young Garlock received through a dream a clear call to missionary service. He knew God did not want his life to end; there was more for him to do. And soon, in answer to his parents' fervent prayers, he was on his feet again.

Within a few years of his narrow escape from death, Garlock was forging rivers, enduring famine and oppressive heat, and drinking the typhoid-infested water of untamed Africa. After completing his studies in 1920 at Beulah Height Bible School, H.B. and his sister Blanche determined to sail for Africa. Their parents accompanied them to the ship in New York harbor. They were presenting two children in one day for missionary service.

Liberia, in West Africa, was known as "the white man's grave," because so few missionaries survived the diseases and heat of the region. Also, cannibalism (the terrible practice of eating human flesh) was still practiced by many tribes. Into that difficult area, H.B. and Blanche Garlock settled as missionaries. When the first missionaries had rowed ashore only a few years earlier, an excited African ran to them and said, "I know who you are; you are missionaries! God appeared to me in a dream and told me to come to the coast and meet people who would preach good news to my tribe." Now the Christian message was gaining a foothold in a place bound by centuries of superstition.

In 1921, Garlock married Ruth Trotter, a girl he had fallen in love with in Bible college. They would serve the Lord together for many years, both in Africa and in the United States.

The Liberian people renamed Garlock, Kwi Kali, meaning "white bird." He started a church and opened a mission school in the village of Gropaka. King Jufuli, king of the region, sent his son to the mission school. There, young James heard amazing Bible stories for the first time. One morning, Garlock was reading the story of Jesus' healing blind Bartimaeus. James had cataracts, which caused him to be blind.

Upon hearing this Bible story, James asked if Jesus could make him see as He made Bartimaeus see. Garlock swallowed hard and told James to pray and believe. After a fervent prayer, the cataracts completely disappeared. The young man's face lit up, and he ran all the way into town to his father's house to show him what God had done.[1]

The people of Gropaka had asked for evidence of the power of the God the missionary preached. Now, here was living proof that Jesus was alive. The news spread rapidly, and many people put their faith in Jesus when they saw what had happened to James. King Jufuli renounced his worship of idols and gave his life to Christ, as did most of his counselors.

Garlock continued to see the miraculous power of God at work. Some time after the healing of Jufuli's son, H.B., along with several African helpers, trudged through thick jungle to rescue a young girl who had been kidnapped by another tribe. When he arrived at the tribe's village, he was surrounded by angry people with spears poised to attack. How would he escape? Garlock tells the story:

> They made a mad rush toward me with drawn knives, shouting, "Kill him, kill him!" The leader rushed at me with his cutlass raised to behead me.

When it seemed the end had come and my head was about to be severed from my body, I closed my eyes and committed myself to God, repeating over and over again that one name that is above every name, "Jesus, Jesus!"

Suddenly, there was a deathlike stillness! The tom-toms stopped beating and all screaming and yelling halted abruptly. . . . I cautiously opened my eyes — and wondered if I could believe them. Before me stood some of the savages with their weapons upraised ready to strike, while others held drawn knives by their sides. But all were frozen in their tracks. . . . The God that closed the lions' mouths in Daniel's time had held these wild, angry cannibals at bay!

I have often wondered if they saw the Angel of the Lord. . . . Or perhaps . . . they saw the horses and chariots of fire encircling our little company. One thing was certain — they did feel and see something that caused them to know that God was there protecting His servants. God had performed a miracle before our very eyes.[2]

A few years later, Garlock was again surrounded by an angry tribe of cannibals. The witch doctor threw his wand on the ground before Garlock as if to say, "Before we kill and eat you, you are permitted to speak." Garlock remembered Jesus' words in Mark 13:11: "Do not worry beforehand, or premeditate what you will speak. But whatever is given you in that hour, speak that; for it is not you who speak, but the

Holy Spirit." He opened his mouth and a flood of words poured out that he had never learned. When he had finished, the witch doctor asked forgiveness on behalf of the tribe for trying to harm him. Again, the gospel had triumphed and Kwi Kali's life was spared.

As Garlock was making one of his frequent trips to preach to still another tribe, he saw a mountain that seemed strangely familiar to him. Yet he knew he had never been there before. Then he remembered. He *had* seen this mountain years before. When the Lord had called him to be a missionary when he was so ill with influenza as a teenager, He had shown him *this mountain* and assured the fever-ridden boy he would bring God's message to the people there. Now, years later, God fulfilled the promise.

Garlock would go to other missions works in Ghana and Malawi. He would pastor churches back in America in New Jersey, Colorado, and Kansas. In later years, he became the first field director for Africa for the Assemblies of God. But he would always remember that God spared his life so he could share God's love with even more people.

LET'S BE WORLD CHRISTIANS

H.B. Garlock took great risks to get the gospel to tribes who had never heard of Jesus. Are there risks today in sharing the message of Christ?

LET'S PRAY

Some missionaries experience amazing deliverance from danger, as H.B. Garlock did. Others are tortured and even killed. Let's pray that, like the three Hebrew children, whether or not God spares us from cruelty and death, we will always be true to Him.

7

THE FIRST AMERICAN MISSIONARIES

ADONIRAM JUDSON
(1788–1850)

LET'S REMEMBER

*All authority has been given to Me in heaven
and on earth. Go therefore and make disciples of all
nations, baptizing them in the name of the Father
and of the Son and of the Holy Spirit, teaching them
to observe all things that I have commanded you; and
lo, I am with you always, even to the end of the age*
(Matt. 28:18–20).

LET'S LISTEN

Few missionaries have ever had it tougher than Adoniram
Judson. During his missionary service, he experienced the death
of two wives and several children, battled frequent bouts of fever, and was brutally treated in a death prison for 17 months.

In spite of all these sorrows, Judson still made one of the greatest impacts for Christ in history. In addition to his preaching ministry, Judson left the lasting treasures of several Bible revisions and translations and an English-Burmese dictionary.

Adoniram Judson was born in 1788 in Massachusetts, the son of a minister in the Congregational church. Judson always excelled in school. When barely 16, he entered Brown College, graduating as valedictorian of his class after only three years.

Judson's inquiring mind caused him to ask hard questions about the Christian faith of his parents. At this time, he had not yet made a firm commitment to God. Nevertheless, after college he enrolled in the new Andover Theological Seminary.

Several events during this time brought Judson to a commitment to Christ. In a bizarre circumstance, while he was staying in a village inn, he heard the screams of a dying man in the room next to his. The next morning, he learned that the screams came from a close college friend who had died. This deeply affected Judson, and he began to seek answers about the Lord instead of asking more questions.

At Andover, he met Samuel Mills, who a few years earlier had spearheaded the famous "haystack prayer meeting" at Williams College. Some historians marked this unplanned outdoor prayer meeting as the true beginning of the missionary movement in America. While taking shelter from the rain under a haystack, several students pledged themselves to missionary service. They believed their commitment could spark the fulfillment of the Great Commission. "We can do it, if we will," they encouraged each other. Through his ongoing friendship with Judson, Mills was a key factor in pointing Judson to the mission fields of the world.

During his years of seminary, Judson dedicated his life to the Lord and to world missions. With Samuel Mills, Judson helped form the American Board of Commissioners for Foreign Missions. In 1812, Judson and his new wife, Nancy, boarded ship as the first American missionaries. They first disembarked in India, but circumstances pointed them toward Burma. Landing in Rangoon, they teamed with William Carey's son Felix to reach the Burmese with the gospel. They immediately set out to learn the difficult language, often studying 12 hours a day.

Judson and Nancy searched for new ways to reach the people. They realized the Burmese did not respond well to church buildings like those in Western countries. They also observed that people thronged the local *zayats*, open areas for discussion and meditation. Between bouts of fever, the Judsons raised money and built a zayat for the purpose of sharing the gospel. Their plan worked, and soon there were several inquirers who became followers of Jesus Christ.

Their work was interrupted when war broke out between Burma and England. The Burmese government suspected all foreigners as spies and sentenced them all to prison. Judson's pleading that he was an American, not English, and had nothing to do with the military actions of England, fell on deaf ears, and he was sent to a Burmese death prison, a place for prisoners sentenced to die. As the British advanced, the prisoners were driven northward. After over a year of no exercise and little nourishment, the march proved too much for many of the prisoners. Several died on the way. Although Judson survived the journey, he never fully recovered physically.

Sorrows mounted for Adoniram Judson. By 1826, Nancy and two of their children had died. In 1845, his second wife died. His work kept him away from home, and he experienced the agony of being separated often from his children.

Nevertheless, after a period of deep discouragement, new power from the Holy Spirit surged through Judson and he was refreshed to continue his preaching. In 1840, 28 years after landing in Burma, Judson completed his translation of the Burmese Bible and sent it to the press. Returning to America on furlough, he was afforded a hero's welcome. His name had become a household word among Christians. However, Judson was uncomfortable with this notoriety. He often disappointed his American audiences because he did not tell exciting missionary stories; instead, he preached the gospel.

While in America, he met and married Emily Chubbock, who returned with him to Burma. A gifted writer, she helped him complete a Burmese dictionary in 1849. Emily was expecting their second child when Judson became seriously ill. He left on a voyage, hoping to recover. But he died on the journey and was buried at sea.

Despite the illness and death of family members, Judson held to his faith in God. He never lost sight of his vision to evangelize Burma. As he stood against great odds, he was able to say, "The prospects are as bright as the promises of God."[1]

LET'S BE WORLD CHRISTIANS

Judson used the *zayat*, something familiar to the people, to break through barriers. What ways would you use in another country to help the people feel at ease around you?

LET'S PRAY

Adoniram Judson used his brilliant mind to leave a lasting, valuable contribution to Burma: a Bible and a dictionary. Let's dedicate our minds to God for His service.

8

THE FLYING
SCOT

ERIC LIDDELL
(1902–1945)

LET'S REMEMBER

> *I press toward the goal for the prize of the up-
> ward call of God in Christ Jesus* (Phil. 3:14).

LET'S LISTEN

Why would Hollywood be interested in making a film about a missionary from Scotland, 35 years after his death? Why did that film, *Chariots of Fire*, capture the hearts of millions and become the Academy Award-winning picture of the year? What is so special about Eric Liddell?

Eric Liddell lived for Christ without compromise in the 20th century. Born of missionary parents in Tientsin, China, he later became the most popular and most widely known athlete Scotland had ever produced. A champion rugby player for Scotland's national team, he finally concentrated on his God-given ability to run.

Liddell's perseverance and commitment to Christ was evident throughout his athletic career. In an international contest in 1923, he was forced off the track as the runners scrambled for position in the 440-yard run. By the time he got up, the other runners were 20 yards ahead. With amazing determination, he caught up, then passed the other runners. He came in first and collapsed just across the finish line.

Liddell made world news in the 1924 Olympic Games in Paris. When it was announced that the heats of the 100 meters were to be held on Sunday, he refused to run. The Sabbath was to be devoted to the Lord, not to sports, Liddell said. Even those who did not agree with him admired this young man's unshakable convictions. Liddell chose to run the 400 meters instead, and even though he drew the outside lane, the hardest lane for that race, he won the race and the gold medal.

This world record holder was hailed as a national hero on his return to Scotland. He spent the next year as an effective evangelist, traveling throughout Britain and America. This world-famous man then quietly slipped out of the spotlight to pursue his life's call to China.

Affiliated with the London Missionary Society, he taught at the Anglo-Chinese College in Tientsin for a number of years. Then he accepted the hard challenge of rural evangelism, which often required many miles of travel by foot and bicycle under rugged conditions.

Liddell always showed compassion for the people to whom he ministered. After Japan's army occupied a province in China, Liddell helped to care for those wounded in the fighting. Several Chinese men were sentenced by the Japanese soldiers to be beheaded. One man refused to kneel to the swift swish of the soldiers' swords. The sword missed its mark, inflicting a deep gash from the back of the man's head to his mouth. He was left for dead. But Eric found the terribly wounded man and pulled him in a cart 18 miles to a mission hospital. Not only did the man live, but he became a follower of Jesus Christ.

Eric's athletic talents did not go unnoticed during his missionary career. Once, he was asked to run a race at an athletic meet in north China. He took it as an opportunity to testify to his faith in Jesus Christ. The crowd was so pleased at how he outdistanced the other runners that they persuaded him to run an extra race. What the crowd did not know was that Liddell's boat was due to leave in just a few minutes.

Having won the second race, Eric was about to leap into a waiting taxi when the playing of the national anthem forced him to stand at attention. He then jumped into the taxi, which sped across town, reaching the wharf just as the boat was moving out from the dock. A wave lifted the boat nearer to the dock, and Eric threw his bags on board, took a great leap, and landed on the departing boat!

Although Eric was devoted to getting the gospel to those who had not heard it, he also wanted to see Christians grow in their walk with the Lord. "The Christian life should be a life of growth," he said. "I believe the secret of growth is to develop the devotional life."[1]

In 1942, the Chinese province where Liddell served as a missionary was overrun by the invading Japanese. All foreign inhabitants, including missionaries and missionary children, were put in prison camps. Eric made the welfare of each prisoner his concern, even to the point of injuring his own health. He continued to preach Christ to the 1,800 people who were jammed into the camp, which measured only 150 by 200 yards. He encouraged the prisoners with his favorite Bible passages in 1 Corinthians 13 and Matthew 5. And he taught them to trust God through that ordeal with the words of a well-loved hymn:

> Be still, my soul: the Lord is on thy side;
> Bear patiently the cross of grief or pain;
> Leave to thy God to order and provide;
> In every change He faithful will remain.
> Be still, my soul: thy best, thy heavenly Friend
> Through thorny ways leads to a joyful end.[2]

Liddell became "Uncle Eric" to the missionary children, bolstering their courage by leading them in games. One man who survived the harsh camp as a child later said, "None of us will ever forget this man whose humble life combined muscular Christianity with radiant godliness. What was his secret? He unreservedly committed his life to Jesus Christ as Savior and Lord. That friendship meant everything to him."[3]

Liddell's wife, Florence, had been taken to safety in Canada. There she gave birth to their third daughter, whom Eric never saw.

Liddell died of a brain tumor in the prison camp shortly before he was to be released. A leading newspaper in Scotland wrote, "Scotland has lost a son who did her proud every hour of his life."

A fitting tribute was given at the end of *Chariots of Fire*:

Eric Liddell, missionary,
Died in occupied China
At the end of World War II.
All of Scotland mourned.

LET'S BE WORLD CHRISTIANS

Eric Liddell used athletics as a platform to preach Christ to many who otherwise would not be interested. What talent do you have that can help draw people to Jesus?

LET'S PRAY

Liddell put personal convictions above fame. He was willing to give up a chance for Olympic gold, after training for years, to be true to his commitment to God. Pray that the approval of the Lord will be more important to you than the praises of people.

9

THE STUDENTS' FRIEND

PAUL LITTLE
(1928–1975)

LET'S REMEMBER

> *But in your hearts set apart Christ as Lord. Always be prepared to give an answer to everyone who asks you to give the reason for the hope that you have. But do this with gentleness and respect* (1 Pet. 3:15–16; NIV).

LET'S LISTEN

Paul Little became a symbol for college students because of his joyful style of sharing his faith in Christ with others. Everywhere he went, his message was received with enthusiasm, especially by America's Christian college students in the sixties and seventies. It seemed his life was cut short when, at the age of 46, on a well-deserved family vacation in Canada, he died in a traffic accident. But he is now more alive than ever as his ministry continues through his writings, recorded messages, and the people to whom he personally ministered during his life. He may now be reaching more people than ever before.

Paul Little was born December 30, 1928, to a devout Plymouth Brethren family in Upper Darby, Pennsylvania. The Plymouth Brethren have produced many famous Bible scholars, including H.A. Ironside and J.N.N. Darby. Because of the strong Christian influence in his home, it is no surprise that Paul became a Christian at an early age. Paul Little gave his heart to Christ on January 1, 1937, at the age of 8, but fully committed his life to Christ at age 13. Looking back, he said, "I knew the gospel from year one, through assembly meetings, Sunday school, and the reading of Scripture every day at home."

While still a teenager, Paul discovered that he had a heart condition which would probably prevent his entering the Christian ministry. So he determined to become a business-man. He enrolled in the Wharton School of Finance at the University of Pennsylvania, from which he received a bach-elor of science degree.

While at Penn, he was active in the Inter-Varsity chapter, a group of Christian students meeting on his campus. When Little graduated in 1950, Joseph Bayle, a renowned Christian writer, asked Little to become an Inter-Varsity staff member. "It's one of the best things I ever did for the Christian wit-ness in our universities and in the United States," Bayle said later.

Little was given an assignment for Inter-Varsity in New York City in 1953. There he met and began to date Marie

Huttenlock, a former China Inland Missionary. She had been reassigned to minister to the 5,000 Chinese students who were stranded in New York as a result of the Korean War. Paul and Marie were later married.

Paul Little's ministry was wide and varied. He was always helpful to students, especially to those who struggled to know God's will for their lives. Students lauded his speaking style and sense of humor. Although Paul emphasized the importance of winning people to Christ, he also urged people to develop a growing devotional life. Addressing students at a missions conference, Paul said, "If you wait to *find* time, you will never find it. You have to *take* the time."

Little received a master of arts in biblical literature at Wheaton College and, in 1964, became assistant professor of evangelism in the School of World Missions at Trinity Evangelical Divinity School. Since his death, the Paul Little Chair of Evangelism has been established at Trinity.

Little was a great crusader for foreign missions. His leadership in the Urbana Conventions and at the International Congress on World Evangelization in Lausanne, Switzerland, will always be remembered. Not only did Paul serve as assistant director and director of the Urbana gatherings, which are held every three years, but he was also a frequent speaker at the meetings. Little challenged thousands of students to consider foreign missions as their life work.

Billy Graham asked Paul Little if he would be the assistant program director for the International Congress for World Evangelization in 1974. After praying about it, Little accepted. He became very excited about this gathering of international church leaders, and he encouraged the participants to keep their eyes on the single great task of reaching the world with the gospel: "The tide is in for . . . witness around the world and the (feeling) was we should move on that tide toward the goal of world evangelization in this century."

Perhaps his most lasting contribution is contained in his writings. He authored three books: *How to Give Away Your Faith, Know Why You Believe,* and *Know What You Believe.* He also wrote several booklets and articles.

Paul Little set a tone for a style of evangelism that was both gracious and straightforward. In *How to Give Away Your Faith*, he urged Christians to be involved with non-Christians without compromising their Christian faith. He defended the truth that Jesus Christ is the only way to God, and only through Him can we have forgiveness of sins.

Little wrote an article only a few months before his death titled, "The God Who Never Lets Things Just Happen." In it he wrote, "The apostle Paul wasn't looking to death as a cop-out, but rather as a fulfillment of the ministry God had given him. He had confidence in God for the future, whatever it might be. Your future and mine are uncertain, too . . . nothing happens by accident, and we can rest with confidence in that."[1]

LET'S BE WORLD CHRISTIANS

Paul Little gave much of his life to challenging students to share their faith in Christ. How important is it to be a witness to others while you are still young?

LET'S PRAY

Ephesians 5:16 says that we should be "redeeming the time, because the days are evil." For Paul Little, life on this planet was short. Let's pray that we will live all our days for Jesus.

10

THE SMOKE OF A THOUSAND VILLAGES

DAVID LIVINGSTONE
(1813–1873)

LET'S REMEMBER

> But He said to them, "Let us go into the next towns, that I may preach there also, because for this purpose I have come forth" (Mark 1:38).

LET'S LISTEN

"God had an only Son and He made Him a missionary." These words, attributed to David Livingstone, revealed his passion for missions. Although Livingstone was an explorer, doctor, author, and cartographer (a person who charts maps), his enduring fame is as a missionary. In fact, David Livingstone is probably the most famous missionary of all time.

Born in humble surroundings in Blantyre, Scotland, in 1813, by the age of ten he was working up to ten hours a day in the textile mills. With his first earnings, he bought a Latin grammar book. Even though his education was sometimes hampered because he had to work, Livingstone had a thirst for knowledge. He took night courses and read medical journals and his Bible by the dim lights in the mills. He eventually received a degree in medicine and theology from Anderson's College, a part of Glasgow University.

Brought up in a strict Calvinistic faith, David joined an independent Christian congregation of even stricter discipline when he was 17. When he was 21, an appeal by British and American churches for qualified medical missionaries in China made him determined to become one. Then one night he heard a missionary challenge by the famous missionary Robert Moffat, who would one day become his father-in-law. Moffat, who had served along the coastline of southern Africa, challenged his audience to share God's love in "the vast plain to the north" where he had "sometimes seen, in the morning sun, the smoke of a thousand villages, where no missionary had ever been."

Livingstone later recalled, "I saw the duty and inestimable privilege *immediately* to accept salvation by Christ. Humbly believing that through sovereign mercy and grace I have been enabled to do so . . . it is my desire to show my attachment to the cause of Him who died for me by devoting my life to His service."[1]

In 1840, Livingstone was ordained as a missionary, and the next year set sail for Africa to meet his destiny as a dedicated Christian, a courageous explorer, and a fervent anti-slavery advocate.

Arriving in South Africa, he pushed his search for converts into northern territory where no white man had ever been. Trying to establish a mission station, he was mauled by a lion and suffered intense injury to his arm. Another accident made the injury worse, so he could never again support the barrel of a gun with his left hand.

Livingstone experienced many other adventures. He was the first white man to see Lake Ngami and the magnificent waterfalls of the Zambezi River, which he named after his queen, Victoria Falls. He hoped that the Zambezi, which he called "God's highway into the interior," could be navigated. Livingstone had witnessed the horrors of uncaring merchants capturing and selling Africans. Perhaps navigation of the Zambezi would result in a combination of "commerce and Christianity" which would end the ugly slave trafficking.

In 1845, Livingstone married Robert Moffat's daughter, and she accompanied him on many of his journeys. Her health and the need to provide security and education for their four children finally made it necessary for them to go home to England.

When Livingstone returned to England in 1856 after 16 years in Africa, he received a hero's welcome. While there, he wrote *Missionary Travels and Researches in South Africa*, which became an instant best seller, earning him even more fame throughout the civilized world. The next year, he made an impassioned plea to the young men of Cambridge University to join the missionary movement, especially in Africa. As a result, the Church Missionary Union at Cambridge was formed.

Livingstone returned to Africa to continue his explorations and his evangelistic work. In 1865, after another speaking trip through Britain on behalf of missions, he returned to Africa for the last time. When he disappeared into the

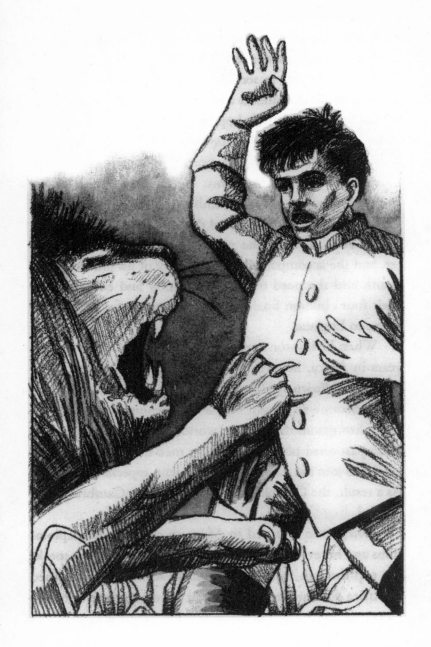

~ Heaven's Heroes ~

heart of the continent, he did not see another European for almost seven years. Rumors spread that Livingstone had been captured or that he had died. In 1871, a famous American newspaper, the *New York Herald*, commissioned H.M. Stanley to go to Africa to find Livingstone.

An amazing set of circumstances eventually brought Stanley and Livingstone face to face in the thick of the African jungle. As they stared at each other, Stanley broke the silence with the now-famous words, "Dr. Livingstone, I presume."

During the next few days, Stanley urged the ill and aging Livingstone to return home with him. Stanley reminded him that he was world-famous, that his books were now classics, and that he could receive medical treatments for his diseases.

Livingstone declined. He had made a commitment to the Lord to both live and die in Africa. Weary, yet still committed to his task, he wrote these words in his journal: "My Jesus, my king, my life, my all. Once more I dedicate my whole self to Thee."

On May 1, 1873, the African helpers found David Livingstone dead, kneeling by his bed in a posture of prayer. Before his death, Livingstone had instructed his helpers to remove his heart from his body and bury it in Africa. His remains were then sent back to England where he was buried in honor in Westminster Abbey.

Someone has said that not only did David Livingstone discover Africa, he discovered the African. His reports on the evil of slavery helped make it illegal throughout the civilized world.

Today, Livingstone's passion for those who had not heard the gospel challenges a new generation of missionary pioneers. The David Livingstone Missionary Foundation is involved in Christian acts of mercy throughout the world. In keeping with the compassion of Livingstone, "the smoke from a thousand villages" drives them on.

LET'S BE WORLD CHRISTIANS

The first years of the 21st century are much different from the days when David Livingstone was alive. Sometimes, missionaries are not allowed to go into places where Jesus' name is not known. But we can still be pioneer missionaries! We can "go" by praying and by giving to Christian preachers who live in that area. Where are some places where Jesus' light is dim that you must "go" by praying and giving?

LET'S PRAY

Pray for missionaries and national preachers who are going into areas that have not heard the message of Jesus.

11

A CHRISTMAS GIFT FOR JESUS

LOTTIE MOON
(1840–1912)

LET'S REMEMBER

> *How then shall they call on Him in whom they have not believed? And how shall they believe in Him of whom they have not heard? And how shall they hear without a preacher? And how shall they preach unless they are sent?* (Rom. 10:14–15).

LET'S LISTEN

If one word was used to describe Lottie Moon, it might well be courage. As a single woman, she overcame great obstacles to bring the message of Christ to the people of north China. During her lifetime, her writings were a strong influence for missions in women's prayer groups in America. But the impact of her life has been far greater since her death.

Lottie was raised in a strong Christian home with the benefits of a good education. One night during college, a campus revival meeting brought her to total commitment to Christ. "I went to the service to scoff," she recalled, "and returned to my room to pray all night."[1]

Her sister Edmonia was one of the first two single women missionaries to be commissioned by the Southern Baptist Convention. But Lottie Moon would be the name that would be endeared to missions-minded Christians for years to come. After college, Lottie helped run the plantation where she was raised, and then became a school teacher in Georgia. But in her heart, she longed to become a missionary. Because her other sisters had served as doctors, business executives, and even in military operations, Lottie did not believe that being a woman would hinder her effectiveness as a missionary. She was right. In 1873, one year after her sister Edmonia, Lottie Moon sailed for China.

Lottie's missionary commitment always came first. An old boyfriend, who was by then a professor, had proposed to her. Although Lottie had strong feelings for him, she could not endorse his belief in evolution. This disagreement was serious enough for Lottie to refuse his marriage proposal. Years later, Lottie was asked if she ever considered marriage. "Yes," she said, "but God had first claim on my life, and since the two conflicted, there could be no question about the result."[2]

In many ways, Lottie was ahead of her time. She insisted that women should have the same privileges and responsibilities as men in missions work. Believing it was God's will, Lottie established a church in the section of north China where she had been stationed. Lottie was also ahead of her time in her belief that the new church be "as free from foreign interference

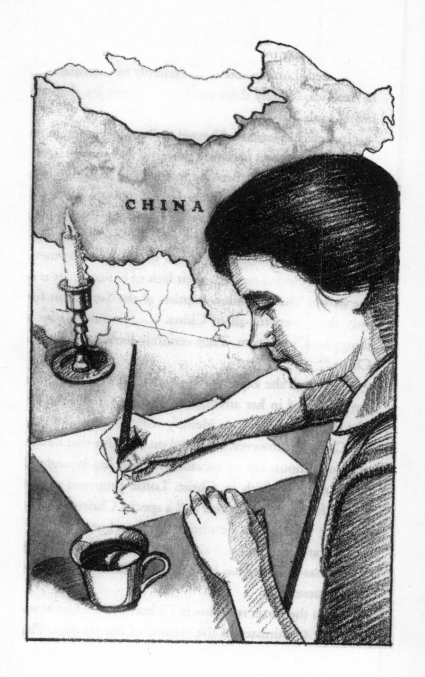

as possible." Over the next two decades, the church Lottie had started saw over a thousand people come to Christ and be baptized. Lottie wrote back excitedly to Christian women in America, "Surely there can be no deeper joy than that of saving souls."[3]

Indeed, her letters addressed to Baptist women in America's southern states became a powerful tool for missions. She urged the women to become involved in missions through their prayers and gifts. These fervent written pleas for the world's masses without Christ became the prayer focus of Baptist Women's Missionary Unions across the South. And while Lottie addressed her letters to Christian women, she sometimes chided men for their lack of concern. "It is odd," she wrote, "that a million Baptists of the South can furnish only three men for all of China. . . . I wonder how these things look in heaven. They certainly look very [strange] in China."[4]

Although she experienced some successes, Lottie was often frustrated in her attempts to win the Chinese to Christ. She found it difficult to identify with and communicate to the Chinese. However, she acted on one idea that has helped send out thousands of missionaries and has brought thousands more to faith in Christ. Lottie proposed a week of prayer for foreign missions and a special Christmas missions offering throughout Southern Baptist churches. The proposal was accepted, and since her death, the Lottie Moon Christmas Offering has brought in millions of dollars yearly for missions.

After the Boxer rebellion in China in 1900, Lottie worked tirelessly to minister to the victims of the conflict. Plagues, smallpox, famine, and local fighting brought mass starvation to the Tengchow area where Lottie worked, and she drained her life's savings attempting to help the Chinese. Her health weakened and friends urged her to return to the States for medical treatment. She died on a ship returning to America on Christmas Eve 1912, one week after her 72nd birthday.

Today, Lottie Moon is the most famous Southern Baptist missionary, and her memory continues to stir the hearts of Christians to give through the Christmas offering for the advance of the gospel. People cannot go as missionaries unless they are sent by the prayers and giving of concerned Christians. Lottie Moon, without knowing it, has been responsible for sending out thousands of missionaries around the world.

LET'S BE WORLD CHRISTIANS

Jesus said, "For where your treasure is, there your heart will be also" (Matt 6:21). Why, then, is it so important to give our money to missions?

LET'S PRAY

Like Lottie, we may sometimes think we are failing when we are actually influencing generations yet unborn. Perhaps just one "little idea" God gives you will help spread the message of Jesus around the world. Let's pray that God will give us fresh, new ideas that will be used for His glory.

12

WORLD MISSIONARY STATESMAN

JOHN R. MOTT
(1865–1955)

LET'S REMEMBER

That they all may be as one, as You, Father, are in Me, and I in You; that they also may be one in Us, that the world, may believe that You sent Me (John 17:21).

LET'S LISTEN

John R. Mott had been called "the most influential religious leader of the 20th century." His influence was perhaps even more widespread than that of his hero, David Livingstone. From the time he was a young person, Mott said, "I have never been disappointed."

To many in our time, however, John R. Mott is largely forgotten. Who was he? Why was he such a force for missions?

John R. Mott was born in New York and raised in Iowa by God-fearing parents. He learned the message of the gospel in his home at a Methodist family altar. Later, as a college student at Cornell, he committed his life to Christ under the preaching of J.E.K. Studd, brother of the famous missionary C.T. Studd. One night, Mott slipped into a meeting just in time to hear Studd issue the challenge, "Young man, seekest thou great things for thyself? Seek them not! Seek ye first the kingdom of God." Mott took the challenge personally and from that time gave himself to the cause of Christ.

In 1886, he represented his college at the Christian Student Conference at Mount Hermon, sponsored by D.L. Moody. There, along with 100 other students, he signed the "Princeton Pledge," which stated, "I purpose, God willing, to become a foreign missionary."

Soon Mott was actively engaged in Christian endeavors. In 1888, he became the general secretary of the Student YMCA, which, at that time, gave priority to winning young men to faith in Christ. That same year, at the age of 23, he became the chairman of the Student Volunteer Movement (SVM) for Foreign Missions. Over the years he would be the driving force behind the SVM, which sent some 20,000 young people into the missionary ranks. Their rallying cry was "the evangelization of the world in this generation."

Mott explained his concept of missions this way:

> It is not necessary that we go to the Scriptures, or to the ends of the earth, to discover our obligation to the unevangelized. A knowledge of our own hearts should be sufficient to make plain

our duty. We know our need of Christ. How un-
reasonable, therefore, for us to assume that the nation living in sin and wretchedness and bondage
can do without Him whom we so much need even
in the most favored Christian lands.[1]

The highlight of Mott's remarkable career as a voice for
missions came in 1910 when he helped convene and preside
over the World Missionary Conference at Edinburgh, Scotland. This conference, with 1,355 delegates, was the first
inter-church conference on missions in modern times.

Mott continued to be a major voice for missions. He always challenged young people to take Christ's message to the
whole world. "The worldwide proclamation of the gospel
awaits accomplishment by a generation which shall have the
obedience, courage, and determination to attempt the task,"
he said.[2]

He was chairman of several influential missionary coun-
cils, including the International Missionary Council and the
Conference of Missionaries to Muslims in 1928. Then in
1948 he was named co-president of the newly formed World
Council of Churches. Mott was a pioneer in helping to bring
together churches and denominations.

Throughout his life, Mott worked for unity and cooperation among Christians. He believed a united Christian
witness was vital for effective evangelism and missions. Although he remained a Methodist layman, his wise council
was sought by church leaders, presidents, and government
officials worldwide. In 1946, he was awarded the Nobel
Peace Prize for his work in reconciling individuals, churches,
and nations.

Although he traveled tirelessly, Mott was a devoted family man. Leila, his wife for 62 years, often traveled with him, challenging young women to become missionaries, and ministering to missionary wives.

On January 31, 1955, John R. Mott died, passing his torch of world evangelization to others. Although he was the friend of kings and presidents, he viewed himself first as a soul winner. "While life lasts," Mott said, "I am an evangelist."

LET'S BE WORLD CHRISTIANS

When we think of John R. Mott, we immediately think of leadership. Why do you think he was such a great leader?

LET'S PRAY

Mott longed for Christians to work together to bring the world to Christ. Look again at John 17:21. Then pray Jesus' prayer for His followers "that they also may be one . . . that the world may believe" in Christ.

13

THE THINGS THAT BREAK GOD'S HEART

BOB PIERCE
(1914–1978)

LET'S REMEMBER

> *For the love of Christ compels us, because we judge thus: that if One died for all, then all died; and He died for all, that those who live should live no longer for themselves, but for Him who died for them and rose again* (2 Cor. 5:14–15).

LET'S LISTEN

Bob Pierce witnessed firsthand the horrors of the Korean War's effects on Korea's children. Deeply moved, he wrote in his Bible, "Let my heart be broken by the things that break the heart of God."

Little did Bob Pierce know the great cost that would be involved in the fulfillment of that prayer. But he did know that indelibly etched on his mind were the effects of the Korean War, where he had seen unclaimed children eating out of trash cans and sleeping under cardboard. Bob himself would suffer tremendous heartache — several illnesses, wrenching disagreements with friends, and the tragic loss of one of his daughters. But his commitment to helping others in pain led him to establish two great Christian caring ministries: World Vision and Samaritan's Purse. They were born, as one friend said, not so much as organizations but as the spurting blood from Pierce's broken heart.

Bob Pierce was born in Iowa in 1914. His godly parents encouraged him from birth to serve the Lord and lead a holy life. So it is not surprising that Bob came to Christ as a child. He was called to preach the gospel when he was 12. Bob's father died that same year. Through the grief, Bob remained committed to Christ, even though he stumbled along the way. He later recalled, "From that time at age 12, I've sinned, I've quit, I've failed, I've stumbled, I've fallen, I've landed in the mud puddle and come out drenched with mud. But one thing has been true: God set me apart and there's no way that I could run away from God. I have tried."[1]

After a time of study at Pasadena Nazarene College, he was ordained to the ministry. Soon afterward he met Lorraine Johnson, the daughter of a noted pastor in the Nazarene church. Bob and Lorraine were married and three daughters were born from this union. Their life was often hard and filled with many goodbyes, as Bob was off for another missionary journey. But the sacrifices of the Pierce family brought rich rewards to people around the world.

Bob was on the ground floor of the Youth for Christ ministry to Asia while Billy Graham opened YFC in Britain.

Bob was involved with the movement because of its strong emphasis on winning young people to Christ.

While he will probably be most remembered for his Christian acts of kindness, Bob's drive was as a soul winner and evangelist. "I never wanted to be a famous anything. The passion of my soul since the day God called me . . . the *one thing* — has been that I wanted to see people come to the experience of being born again."[2] Bob knew that would be costly. His prayer in Korea for a broken heart was certainly answered. On his trip for Youth for Christ to the Orient, he felt he had to do something to relieve the suffering he saw everywhere, especially among the precious children. Of this time he later reflected, "The only measurement . . . I had in assessing what we should be in was, *Is this something Jesus would do? Something God would want done?*"[3]

Returning to the States, he launched a ministry dedicated to meeting emergency needs in crisis areas. The first project would be to sponsor the needs for education and basic care for thousands of Korean children. The result was World Vision. Today, this ministry is one of the largest Christian organizations in the world, in the name of Christ helping needy people around the world.

As founder and president of World Vision, Bob established an international relief program to help hungry, desperate children. As his heart had always gone out to pastors in other countries, he established conferences for these brave national church leaders. He organized tours for the Korean Orphans Choir, who sang their way into the hearts of thousands of Americans.

Those who knew Bob Pierce well often spoke of his unusual prayer life. He was constantly, earnestly praying. Much of the time he lived on the edge of a need for a miracle because his huge heart of compassion committed him and his organization to send money that simply was not available. Time after time, he responded to emergency needs of missionaries, then his prayer and faith went to work. He lived in what he called "God room," that area of faith where man's best efforts could not possibly resolve the situation. When the miracles came, only God could get the credit.

One of the first crossroads of faith he faced was when he obeyed God's leading for his initial visit to China. Not having enough money to buy a ticket to China, he went to the airport and purchased a ticket to Honolulu. Then he made a phone call to a friend. When the friend found out that Bob was on his way to Hawaii and was trusting God to provide the needed money to China, he offered to help raise funds for the rest of the trip and to wire the money to him in Honolulu. Bob had made that all-important first step of obedience, and the rest of his needs were met.

Bob traveled the world over, giving hope to the discouraged — and many times the most discouraged were missionaries.

He served much time in Taiwan and Korea, and ministered to the American military in Vietnam. His radio broadcasts from the field to donors in America were some of the finest missionary broadcasts ever produced. Many people found that they read his letters of appeal through eyes blurred with tears. Bob, always a pioneer, also helped begin Great Commission Films, one of the first major Christian film ministries.

Bob Pierce drove himself for the Great Commission. Today, we would say that he suffered burnout. He often worked

himself past the point of physical and emotional exhaustion. Someone said he seemed to absorb all the pain he saw into his own body. Yet, even in his weakened condition, he remained true to the Lord and His calling. "The secret of lasting success," Bob often said, "is lasting!"

After a conflict within the organization, Bob resigned as president of World Vision in 1967. Then, having regained a measure of his health, Bob formed Samaritan's Purse, a smaller ministry dedicated to ministering quickly to crisis situations.

Recognized as a Christian ambassador all over the world, he often was received by heads of state. Nevertheless, he longed for young Christians to see their high calling, saying, "We need men and women . . . who are humble before God, who are aware that their power comes from His indwelling Holy Spirit, and who are confirmed in their minds that God has given them a high calling as His ambassadors. Paul never hung his head before any king but King Jesus."

One of Bob's young "projects" was Franklin Graham, son of evangelist Billy Graham. Today, Franklin is the president of Samaritan's Purse.

Bob Pierce believed in a God of miracles. Once, in Korea, a man tried to disrupt an outdoor meeting where Bob was preaching, by parking a train locomotive close to the meeting and pulling the shrieking whistle every two or three minutes. Bob's response was dramatic. He stood before the audience and challenged the devil:

> I command you, Satan, in the name of Jesus Christ, to still that shrieking whistle and to get that man and his engine out of here at once, so

that people who have never heard the gospel will hear and be saved. And I thank You, Lord, for defeating Satan, and I ask You in the name of Christ to command these demons and whoever they are who have brought this engine and disrupted this meeting to move it out of here and still that thing this very second.[4]

Immediately, the wheels of the train began to move and it backed off, out of sight and sound.

In the mid-1970s, Bob discovered that leukemia was rapidly invading his body. Even then, he did not lessen his pace. In fact, it seemed that he picked up his pace of meeting needs and preaching the gospel. During that time, someone remarked, "Have you heard that Bob Pierce is dying with leukemia?"

The friend replied, "No, he's not. He's *living* with leukemia."

Bob Pierce received numerous awards for his life of service. Three times he was decorated by the Korean government with the highest honor that can be given to a foreigner. He received honorary doctorates from Northwestern School in Minnesota, Yonsei University in Korea, and John Brown University in Arkansas. Yet his greatest reward is in heaven. Many thousands will be there because his love brought them to Jesus.

Bob involved himself in human need wherever he found it. He especially loved helping missionaries, whom he often referred to as heroes of the cross. "I'm not a missionary," he said, "but I own stock in half a dozen projects of one kind or another overseas."

He constantly challenged missionaries and national pastors to give themselves without reserve to Christ: "Most people think what the gospel needs is more clever, skilled people, when what it needs is more people who are willing to bleed, suffer, and die in a passion to see people come to Christ!"[5]

On September 6, 1978, Bob Pierce went home to heaven. Shortly before he died, he said, "I can tell you that, when you are just outside of heaven, all that matters is that you loved and served Jesus."[6]

After his death, tributes to Bob Pierce poured in from around the world. Torrey Johnson, founder of Youth for Christ, said, "I have never met a person with greater compassion." Billy Graham called him a champion of "the 'little people,' the forgotten, the hurting people who are unheard of and unsung except in the courts of heaven." Perhaps the most beautiful tribute was the simple phrase that appeared on the cover of *World Vision* magazine: "Bob Pierce, 1914–1978, Humanity's Friend."

LET'S BE WORLD CHRISTIANS

Why do you think Bob Pierce was so well accepted by governments around the world?

LET'S PRAY

Bob Pierce's famous prayer should never be prayed lightly. Its fulfillment, in some ways, cost him his life. It will go down as one of the greatest, yet simplest, prayers in history: "Let my heart be broken by the things that break the heart of God." Let's ask God for more of His compassion.

14

The Man with a Missionary Heart

Warren Shibley
(1921–1965)

LET'S REMEMBER

> *I will run the course of Your commandments,*
> *For You shall enlarge my heart* (Ps. 119:32).

LET'S LISTEN

Warren Shibley was born in the little Oklahoma town of Drumright on March 4, 1921. His mother's parents had come to America from England, and his father had emigrated from Lebanon as a teenager.

Warren Shibley is a special hero of mine. You see, he's my father. His parents moved to the town of Bristow during the Oklahoma oil boom of the 1920s. Young Shibley, an excellent athlete, was named to the high school all-state teams in both football and basketball.

While he was in high school, Warren's mother experienced a deep spiritual renewal and began to urge him to go with her to church. Soon, Warren had opened his heart to Christ at the church's old-fashioned altar.

Warren was brought up in a patriotic atmosphere. His father, who had witnessed the horrors of civil war and famine before he came to America, was determined to give something back to his adopted country. So he ran for public office and became one of the first immigrants elected to the Oklahoma legislature.

Warren's parents loved America so much that, when he was born, they named him after the president — Warren Harding Shibley.

Upon graduating from high school, Warren declined sports scholarship offers from several major colleges. Instead, he joined the navy. As a sailor during World War II, he saw action in the South Pacific, where his experiences enlarged his heart of compassion and missions vision.

While his shipmates would go out on leave, he would often stay alone on board ship, reading his Bible by a small light above his bunk and praying for a greater heart for the world.

Warren suffered a disability in his feet during the war, and friends urged him to take the disability money that was rightfully his. "My country doesn't owe me anything," he replied, "and I owe it a lot."

After the war, Warren returned home, realizing that his direction in life would never be the same. He could never again hide from the cries of a world that needed Jesus. Soon, he knew that his life must be devoted to getting the good news to others.

In January 1949 he married Lillian Roberts, the secretary of the church he attended. I was their first child, arriving in March the next year. Two sisters followed, in 1955 and 1957.

Warren Shibley was ordained as a minister of the gospel in 1953. In the next 12 years, he would pioneer a nation-wide radio broadcast, start a church and Bible school in Tulsa, publish a monthly missions magazine, and establish the Gleaner Missionary Society. He and my mother also served as founding trustees for the missionary evangelism ministry of T.L. Osborn.

Our home was filled with missionary stories, visits from missionaries and national workers, and evening prayers for God's work worldwide. It was not unusual for me to awaken in the middle of the night to hear my father earnestly praying for nations and missionary friends.

He kept a relentless pace in his desire to see the gospel advanced, and he died at the young age of 44 in 1965. I have only good memories of a man completely committed to the Great Commission. Perhaps, in his zeal, he did not care for his body as he should have, but that verdict is heaven's to give. One thing is certain: Thousands will be in heaven because of his life and heart to minister worldwide.

He left me a rich missions heritage. Each time I board a plane to go somewhere to share Jesus, I remember that I'm reaping the harvest of a life sown to world missions.

He may have known his time was short. I don't know. But he would often recite this reminder to us:

Only one life;
'Twill soon be past.
Only what's done for
Christ will last.

LET'S BE WORLD CHRISTIANS

What lessons are there for us from Warren Shibley's life? Friends referred to him as "the man with a missionary heart." How would you like your friends to remember you?

LET'S PRAY

Like Warren Shibley, we should pray for our friends who serve the Lord as missionaries. Take time now to pray for people you know who are missionaries.

15

BEFORE KINGS AND CHILDREN

MARY SLESSOR
(1848–1915)

LET'S REMEMBER
> *I will speak of Your testimonies also before kings,*
> *And will not be ashamed* (Ps. 119:46).

LET'S LISTEN

Late one night, a ship carrying Mary Slessor and three of her rescued children arrived from Britain in Calibar, West Africa. After disembarking, Mary immediately began walking through the dark, thick jungle with her children toward the missions compound she had established miles inland.

"Weren't you and the children afraid of being attacked by thieves or wild animals?" a friend inquired.

"No self-respecting lion would have dared attack us, the way we sang those hymns!" she replied.

Such was the courage of Mary Slessor, who was born in Dundee, Scotland, into an unhappy, poverty-stricken home. Her alcoholic father sometimes threw young Mary out of the house at night after he had been drinking. Still, she continued to go to school and work with her mother in the mills. By the time she was 14, Mary was the primary wage earner in the family. Her mother could no longer work outside the home, having given birth to her seventh child.

Mary received Christ at an early age and became interested in missions almost immediately. She was active in her Scottish Presbyterian church, teaching Sunday school and working in the church's Queen Street Mission, where she received valuable experience in sharing God's love with needy people.

When Mary was in her twenties, God used two events to lead her to become a missionary. First, Mary's brother John died, deeply grieving the family. Mary's mother had always hoped John would be a missionary. Mary now resolved to take John's place. News of the death of the great missionary-statesman David Livingstone sealed her decision. Here is the story:

> One day, there flashed through the land a telegram which caused much excitement and sorrow. Africa was then an unknown country, vast and mysterious, and haunted by all the horrors of slavery and heathenism. For a long time, there had been tramping through it a white man, a Scotsman, David Livingstone, hero of heroes, who had been gradually finding out the secrets of its lakes and rivers and peoples. Sometimes he was lost for

years. The telegram which came told of his lonely death in a hut in the heart of the continent. Everyone asked: What is to be done now? Who is to take up the work of the great pioneer and help to save the natives from misery and death? Amongst those whose hearts leapt at the call was Mary Slessor.

She went to her mother. "Mother," she said, "I am going to offer myself as a missionary."

Mary Slessor was accepted by the Mission Board of the United Presbyterian Church in Edinburgh to go to Calibar as a teacher. So she who had waited so long and so patiently, working within the walls of a factory, weaving the warp and woof in the loom, was now going to one of the wildest parts of Africa to weave there the lives of the people into new and beautiful patterns.[1]

At age 27, Mary Slessor sailed for Calibar — then part of the British Empire but now part of Nigeria in west Africa. Her first few years of missionary work were trying. Unhappy with her assignment of teaching in the mission school, Mary wanted to meet with people who had not yet heard of Jesus Christ. But tribal customs of witchcraft, superstition, and cruelty prevented the people from being interested in the message of the gospel.

Mary was particularly horrified by the tribal practice of murdering twin babies. The people believed that an evil spirit caused the birth of twins. So they killed the babies and cast out the mother from the tribe.

Mary began to rescue the twin babies and help their homeless mothers. Her involvement endangered her, but eventually led to reform among the tribes. In a letter to a Sunday school class in Dundee, Scotland, she described the moment when she learned the dreadful killings were over:

> Just as it became dark one evening, I was sitting in my verandah talking to the children, when we heard the beating of drums and the singing of men coming near. This was strange, because we were on a piece of ground which no one in the town had a right to enter. Taking the wee twin boys in my hands, I rushed out, and what do you think I saw? A crowd of men standing outside the fence, chanting and swaying their bodies. They were proclaiming that all twins and twin-mothers could now live in the town, and that if anyone murdered the twins or harmed the mothers, he would be hanged by the neck. If you could have heard the twin-mothers who were there, how they laughed and clapped their hands and shouted, "Sosono! Sosono!" (Thank you! Thank you!) You will not wonder that amidst all the noise I turned aside and wept tears of joy and thankfulness, for it was a glorious day for Calibar.
>
> A few days later the treaties were signed, and at the same time a new king was crowned. Twins' mothers were actually sitting with us on the platform in front of all the people.[2]

Mary finally determined to go into a rough, inland area called Okoyong, or the up-country of Calibar. Several missionaries had already been killed in the Okoyong region, and no single woman had ever dared to go there alone. But Mary Slessor was no ordinary person. She would lie awake at night planning ways to get behind the wall of bush. Hundreds of miles inland lay a vast region of forest and river into which white men had not ventured. She knew it would require courage and firmness on her part to combat the savage customs of the people. But Mary had no fear of harm because she wanted more than anything to tell them of Jesus' love for them.

Impressed with her courage, the king of the region helped Mary begin her pioneer missionary work, which continued for the next 25 years. Mary opened schools and medical outposts among the Okoyongs and acted as a judge, helping the people settle their quarrels. She became known as a peacemaker, an example of the words of Jesus: "Blessed are the peacemakers, For they shall be called sons of God" (Matt. 5:9).

Mary Slessor was named the first vice consul of Okoyong in 1892. She came to Calibar as a missionary, and her depth of commitment and willingness to challenge the boundaries of ordinary mission work earned her a position as the first woman vice consul in the British Empire.

Mary remained single throughout her life. She once accepted a marriage proposal from a missionary teacher, but because of his health, her fiancée would not have been able to live in the hardships of 19th century Africa. Mary saw her work for Jesus as more important than marriage, and broke their engagement.

At age 55, Mary pioneered still another missions work in a new, unreached area. She spent the next ten years once again building churches, establishing schools, and telling people the story of Jesus. In 1915, at age 66, she died in a mud hut among the people she loved and served. Her testimony, however, lives on.

LET'S BE WORLD CHRISTIANS

Mary chose missionary work over marriage. Do you think it is worth it to give up life's blessings for others to know about Jesus? Why?

LET'S PRAY

Mary influenced kings and government officials, yet she lived a very simple life among the people. She was not afraid to risk her life for people to know Christ. Ask God to give you influence and courage so people can know Jesus Christ.

16

THE PASSION
FOR SOULS

OSWALD J. SMITH
(1889–1986)

LET'S REMEMBER

> *For God so loved the world that He gave His only*
> *begotten Son, that whoever believes in Him should*
> *not perish but have everlasting life* (John 3:16).

LET'S LISTEN

When I was in high school, shortly after God had called
me to preach, someone gave me a copy of *A Passion for Souls*
by Oswald J. Smith. Each page seared its fire into my heart.
I remember the first time I read Dr. Smith's piercing question, which still haunts me: "Why should anyone hear the
gospel twice until everyone has heard it once?" After meeting
Oswald J. Smith through his writings, my life was never the
same.

One of the highest privileges of my life was meeting with Dr. Smith in person. I'll never forget that spring day in 1982 when I drove to his house in Toronto. Though elderly and bedfast, he had graciously consented to receive me. He greeted me warmly. Then, almost immediately, he asked, "Young man, what are you doing for missions?" I was glad to tell him of my ministry in many nations. Yet, in spite of my involvement, in the presence of this greatest living missionary statesman, I felt exceedingly humbled and that I was not doing enough.

Before I left, I asked him to pray. "Dr. Smith," I requested, "will you pray that your passion for souls will be transmitted to my generation?" His aged hand took mine, and he prayed heaven down to earth. That little bedroom became a cathedral for me that day.

Oswald J. Smith was born in a farmhouse on the plains of Ontario, Canada, on November 8, 1889, the eldest of ten children. He was raised in a God-fearing home where prayers and Bible reading were part of the daily routine. Young Oswald battled many sicknesses. Once, while he was fighting pneumonia, his teacher said this poor lad "would never live to see a mission field." Not only did Oswald J. Smith live, but he lived to be almost 100 years old! And not only did he see a mission field, he preached in 70 countries.

In 1906, while still in his teens, Oswald and his brother went to the great evangelistic campaigns in Toronto being conducted by R.A. Torrey. Dr. Torrey was the godly successor to D.L. Moody, and the second president of Moody Bible Institute. There, Oswald heard the gospel clearly presented. He gladly committed his life and future to Jesus Christ.

Soon he felt a clear call to gospel ministry. He enrolled in Toronto Bible College and did further study at Manitoba College. He also studied at McCormack Seminary in Chicago. Ordained as a Presbyterian minister, he became the associate pastor of Dale Presbyterian Church in Toronto in 1915.

Oswald was already ablaze with a passion to see people won to Christ. "I want Thy plan, O God, for my life," he prayed. "May I be happy and contented whether in the homeland or on the foreign field; whether married or alone, in happiness or sorrow, health or sickness, prosperity or adversity — I want Thy plan, O God, for my life. I want it; oh, I want it!"[1]

During his years at college and seminary, God was weaving a missions vision into Oswald. During his last term in seminary, he attended a missionary meeting where a map of the world was prominently displayed. From the map, he caught a fresh glimpse of the world's need for Christ. He realized that his ministry was to be worldwide. "I must be a missionary to the whole world," he wrote in his journal. "My own dear country calls me — would that I might set it on fire for God. But *the world is my parish. Even if I live in one place, I must reach beyond my local parish to the world.*"

His vision to reach the unreached was also expanded during college when he sold Bibles to the Indians in the vast reaches of the Canadian north country. During this time, he began publishing gospel tracts and writing hymns.

On September 12, 1916, he married Daisy, a young deaconess, active in the ministry of Dale Presbyterian Church in Toronto. The next month he became acting pastor of the church. Oswald's strong commitment to world missions did not sit well with some members of the congregation. Oswald himself longed for a church where missions came first. He often said, "The supreme task of the church is the evangelization of the world."

In a time of prayer in 1919, God gave Oswald a vision for a church that would love all the different peoples of earth. Nine years later, the Peoples Church of Toronto, Canada, was established. Dr. Oswald J. Smith would lead the church through the next four decades as the pastor. Later, his son, Paul Smith, was the capable pastor of the church.

Oswald could not be confined to Toronto. Although he was a loyal church pastor, he viewed the church as his base of ministry, not the entire sphere of his ministry. From its beginning, he led the church in bold annual missions conferences. He was the first to use the "faith promise" method of raising money for missions on a large scale. Always, the challenge he placed before his congregation was that they could help reach the entire world from Toronto. He wrote, "I have seen the vision and for self I cannot live; life is less than worthless till my all I give."

Oswald developed a simple, yet powerful, creed for his church:

> We believe in an unmutilated Bible; salvation through the blood of Christ; entire separation from the world; a Spirit-filled life for Christian service; victory over all known sin through the indwelling Christ; rugged consecration to sacrifical service; practical faith in the sufficiency of Christ for spiritual, temporal, and physical needs; the purifying hope of the Lord's return; and a burning

missionary zeal for the bringing back of the King through world evangelization.[2]

The missions conferences of the Peoples Church drew hundreds, sometimes thousands across North America. For many, it was *the* missions event of the year. In 1976, the church gave over a million dollars to missions, and it has continued to give heavily to missions enterprises.

By the early eighties, over $17 million had been raised and the church was helping support 242 missionaries and 222 national workers. Oswald J. Smith had a unique ability to convey his heart for the world to his people. This is not an easy assignment, as many pastors have discovered. But no one could deny his love for a lost world. "Oh, these teeming multitudes," he exclaimed. "How they have won me!"[3]

His son Paul often spoke of how his father was driven to reach the unreached. "All his strength and energy of body, soul, and mind," Paul said, "had to be channeled, contained. . . . Father had this sense of destiny."[4]

Oswald's 36 books have sold over six million copies and have been translated into 125 languages. He also wrote an amazing 1,200 hymns. "Then Jesus Came" and "The Song of the Soul Set Free" are among his most popular.

Oswald J. Smith received many honors over the years. He attained several honorary doctorates, the first from Asbury College in 1936. He was a member of the Royal Geographical Society, the Royal Society of Literature of the United Kingdom, and the American Society of Composers, Authors, and Publishers. In 1965, the Evangelical Fellowship of Canada was formed with Oswald as first president.

Billy Graham said of him, "Oswald Smith has been a legend in his time. . . . My whole life and my ministry have been touched and directed by Oswald J. Smith."[5]

Nevertheless, even though he had become famous as a missionary statesman, he remained truly humble. Remembering God's goodness, he said, "The longer I live, the more unworthy I feel. The wonder of God's love becomes more overwhelming with the passing years."[6]

In his later years, he retained a rigorous schedule. More and more, he turned his focus to younger preachers. "You can produce only what you yourself are," he challenged them. "More than ever today, we need the unction of the Holy Spirit. . . . When the Holy Spirit takes control in a church, there will be blessing and unity and power. Souls will be saved. The gospel will go out."[7]

LET'S BE WORLD CHRISTIANS

Oswald J. Smith may have made his greatest contribution to missions through the example of his holy, Christ-like life. Is it important for our lives to back up what we say?

LET'S PRAY

Pray that God will give you a passion for souls.

17

From Cricket to Costly Commitment

C.T. Studd
(1862–1931)

LET'S REMEMBER

> *But what things were gain to me, these I have counted loss for Christ. Yet indeed I also count all things loss for the excellence of the knowledge of Christ Jesus my Lord, for whom I have suffered the loss of all things, and count them as rubbish, that I may gain Christ* (Phil. 3:7–8).

LET'S LISTEN

C.T. Studd was born in the lap of luxury. His father, a wealthy retired planter in India, had returned to England and the leisure of Tedworth, the family estate in Wiltshire. Young C.T. was given the best of British education at Eton and Cambridge.

During college, he was captain of the famous Cambridge cricket team, an English sport similar to baseball. Some people thought C.T. was England's greatest cricketer.

In 1877, his father committed his life to Christ at an evangelistic meeting conducted by the famed American evangelist D.L. Moody. The following year, all three of Mr. Studd's sons were converted. C.T. took an interest in foreign missions and, about six months after his conversion, dedicated his life to missionary service at another meeting conducted by Moody.

While a student at Trinity College at Cambridge, his popularity as a cricketer helped him influence other students. Six other Cambridge students answered the call to missions with C.T. Together they became known as the Cambridge Seven and decided to sail to China to work with Hudson Taylor. One newspaper commented, "Never before in the history of missions has so unique a band set out to labor in the foreign field."

Not everyone supported C.T.'s decision to become a missionary. Cambridge students thought C.T. should pursue a career as a professional cricket player. And even members of his family questioned his move to foreign soil. Yet C.T. persisted and sailed for China with the China Inland Mission in 1885. There he met Priscilla Steward, a missionary with the Salvation Army. They were married after a brief courtship and would someday have four daughters, all born in China.

The Studds' mission was difficult. At that time, few people were trying to help those tormented by drug abuse. C.T. could not stand by; he had to help. The Chinese were not receptive, however, and when C.T. and Priscilla stepped outside their house, they were often besieged with angry cursing from the people. But C.T. continued his work with the drug addicts while Priscilla continued her work with women.

Ill health forced C.T. to return to England. While he recuperated, he traveled and preached to masses of students, who flocked to hear him both in Britain and America. Hundreds committed themselves to missionary service. And his efforts influenced the beginning of the Student Volunteer Movement in America.

After six years, he returned overseas, this time to India, where he pastored for several years. Again, he was forced to return home because of illness.

It seemed impossible, however, for C.T. Studd not to be engaged in missionary work. Priscilla was suffering from a heart condition, and C.T. himself was far from healthy. Nevertheless, he struck out again for missionary soil — this time his destination was Africa. This once-wealthy man was now 50 years old, in poor health, and had little financial support. Although he was heir to a large inheritance, he gave it all away to missionary work so he could live as a "faith missionary."

C.T.'s work in central Africa was a mixture of successes and failures. His actions were sometimes questioned, even by his most loyal supporters. He appeared to be overly strict on himself and others. He required the missionaries to live an African lifestyle, avoiding any appearance of European affluence. He called this the cost of full commitment to the Lord and His work. Although his commitment to Christ was a positive influence, his stubborn determination sometimes had negative results. Never relaxing in zeal or in effort, he labored long hours with no breaks, and he had little sympathy for those who did not do the same. This cost C.T. his health as well as the support of fellow missionaries and national workers whom he injured with his insensitive remarks.

No one ever questioned C.T. Studd's unshakable commitment to the task of evangelizing the world. Along with co-worker Norman Grubb, C.T. established the Worldwide Evangelization Crusade (WEC). Today, WEC continues to reach around the globe with hundreds of missionaries.

C.T. Studd saw no sacrifice as too great for the advance of the gospel. He gave up fortune and fame in athletics. He surrendered time with his wife and family. He worked tirelessly, and for all this he was sometimes misunderstood. Yet he never retreated from his missionary call: "If Jesus Christ be God and died for me, then no sacrifice is too great for me to give for Him."

LET'S BE WORLD CHRISTIANS

Do you think it was right for C.T. to work so hard and long? Why do you think he worked as he did?

LET'S PRAY

No person is perfect except Jesus. Even though C.T. Studd made mistakes, we can still take a lesson from his zeal to reach people for Christ. Ask God to give you both zeal and wisdom.

THE
EXCHANGED LIFE

HUDSON TAYLOR
(1832–1905)

LET'S REMEMBER

> *I have been crucified with Christ; it is no longer I who live, but Christ lives in me; and the life which I now live in the flesh I live by faith in the Son of God, who loved me and gave Himself for me* (Gal. 2:20).

LET'S LISTEN

"No other missionary in the 19 centuries since the apostle Paul has had a wider vision and has carried out a more systematized plan of evangelizing a broad geographical area than Hudson Taylor."[1] With the possible exception of David Livingstone, no one life has challenged more people for missionary service.

Hudson Taylor was born in Yorkshire, England, in 1832. His father was a Methodist lay preacher and pharmacist. When he was only five years old, young Hudson believed God wanted him to be a missionary. When amused relatives and friends would ask where, his immediate reply was "China."

God gave Hudson this vivid insight into his future. Yet Hudson did not come into a personal relationship with Jesus Christ until he was 17. After reading a gospel tract, he was intensely convicted of his need for the Savior, and immediately committed his life to Christ. Hudson's mother, away on a two-week trip, was not at all surprised when she returned and heard of his conversion. At the exact hour of his commitment, though miles away, she had been praying for him, deeply burdened. When the burden lifted, she knew Hudson had given his heart to Christ.

Here is how Hudson later described their meeting. "When our dear mother came home a fortnight later, I was the first to meet her at the door, and to tell her I had such glad news to give. She said, 'I know, my boy; I have been rejoicing for a fortnight in the glad tiding you have to tell me.' "[2]

Soon the whisperings in his heart for China returned, more intensely than ever. He began to study medicine, hoping that a medical degree might open China's door to him. He also imposed on himself a sparse diet and rugged lifestyle, believing this would prepare him for the years ahead.

"Having now the twofold object in view of accustoming myself to endure hardness and economizing in order to be able more largely to assist others," he later recalled, "I soon found that I could live upon very much less than I had previously thought possible."[3]

Finally, the day came when he set sail for China, arriving in Shanghai in 1854. But his lofty vision to quickly evangelize China's millions was soon weighted with the discouragements of learning the difficult language, receiving limited support, and enduring disapproval from the older missionaries. Hudson did not give up, however; he had committed himself to God and to this work.

Traveling into the interior of China where no other missionary had gone, he was disappointed to find that the people were more interested in his different dress than in his message. There seemed to be only one solution: he would dress Chinese! Hudson shaved part of his head and braided and dyed his remaining hair. His plan worked! The Chinese began to respond when he told them of Christ.

During this time, he met Maria Dyer. Born of missionary parents in China, she had received her schooling in England, and returned to China in her late teens. Maria's protective teacher, Mrs. Aldersey, did not approve of Hudson's "improper" manners — going against established missionary customs and dressing like the Chinese — and almost ruined their romance. Eventually, the young couple was able to marry on January 20, 1858.

Hudson and his new wife were happy in their joint ministry, but Hudson realized he needed more medical training. This need, along with his weakening health, sent the Taylors back to England for an extended furlough. It proved to be no vacation, however. Hudson often worked up to 15 hours a day, revising the New Testament in the Ningpo language. Habits of discipline and organization, learned years earlier, were now paying off and would be even more valuable in the days ahead.

While in England, Hudson's heart burned more passionately than ever to see the gospel reach every person in China. Therefore, he challenged Christians across England to pray, give, and go to China where "a million souls each month" were going into eternity without Christ. During this time, the vision for the China Inland Mission (CIM) was born in Hudson's heart. In 1865, CIM officially began its ministry. The next year, Hudson left with the largest group of missions recruits ever to set sail up to that time. He reasoned that "twenty-four willing, skillful laborers" would provide the needed manpower to put two missionaries in each unreached province in China.

Disunity almost dashed noble venture. New recruits were offended at having to wear Chinese dress, and questioned Hudson's decision as leader of the new mission. The untimely death of the Taylors' daughter Gracie brought some temporary healing to the strained relations. The discontent was eventually traced to one couple and two sisters. When they left, a cooperative spirit was restored and the China Inland Mission expanded rapidly.

Tragedies multiplied for the Taylors. A young son died. The family went through the pain of the surviving children's departure for England and school. Another baby was born but lived less than two weeks. A few days after his death, Maria died at the age of 33.

On top of these personal sorrows, deep feelings of resentment mounted against the missionaries. Age-old Chinese hostility against foreigners was magnified in the interior. Riots broke out in Yangchow in 1868. The missionaries' home was burned to the ground.

In the midst of this intense pain, Hudson Taylor sought a deeper walk with God. He found the encouragement he

needed in the letter of a friend dated Saturday, September 4, 1869. Hudson's friend urged him to exchange all his weaknesses for the strength of Christ.

He summarized this exchanged life by writing, "To *let* my loving Savior work in me *His will*. . . . Abiding, not striving or struggling. . . . Not a striving to have faith or to increase our faith, but a looking at the faithful One seems all we need."[4] Hudson determined he would learn to abide in Christ and claim his position in Him. He announced, "God has made me a new man."

The following year, Hudson married Jennie Faulding, a 27-year-old missionary. Jenny served the China Inland Mission faithfully, and even led a group of missionary women into an unreached part of the interior.

Hudson Taylor's influence for world evangelization continued to grow. In his own lifetime, he would see CIM dispatch almost 700 missionaries to China. His writings were widely read and his travels brought him wide acclaim. In many ways, he was ahead of his time. He radically identified with the people. He believed the best place to direct the work of missions was in the field, not from a headquarters thousands of miles away. And he helped launch the era of "faith missions," where missionaries trust God for their support. "God's work done in God's way will not lack God's supply," he said.

In 1900, the most terrible slaughter in the history of missions began in China. A decree from Beijing ordered the death of all foreigners. Any hint of Christianity was to be uprooted from the country. One hundred and thirty-five missionaries and 53 missionary children were killed. Those who suffered worst were often CIM missionaries.

By then, Hudson was elderly and trying to regain his

health in Switzerland. The shocking news was almost too much for him. He never fully recovered from the grief. He died one month after returning to his beloved China.

The work that Hudson began, however, continued to grow. In 1964, the China Inland Mission celebrated 100 years of missionary service, and changed its name to the Overseas Missionary Fellowship. It remains today an eloquent testimony to the faith and love for souls that were Hudson Taylor's. Here, indeed, was a rare man.

LET'S BE WORLD CHRISTIANS

Why do you think Hudson Taylor adopted the native dress of the Chinese? What point was he trying to make?

LET'S PRAY

Taylor said, "God's work done in God's way will not lack for God's supply." Let's pray for God's supply for missions works around the world. Then let's listen for how God may wish to use us as His channel of blessing.

19

Does God Speak
My Language?

William Cameron Townsend
(1896–1982)

LET'S REMEMBER

> *You were slain, and have redeemed us to God by*
> *Your blood out of every tribe and tongue and people*
> *and nation* (Rev. 5:9).

LET'S LISTEN

William Cameron Townsend, lovingly known by millions as "Uncle Cam," was ahead of his time with his different approach to mission works. His fresh ideas were not always accepted, however. Through the years, he received both
lavish praise and harsh criticism. Despite disapproval, Uncle
Cam was accepting and tolerant of Christians with opposing
views and of non-Christians. Cam believed that cooperation
among Christians was a must if the Bible was to be translated

into new languages. The message of the Bible would change cultures, he maintained, so getting God's Word to the people was his first concern. Cam's commitment to taking God's Word to those who had never heard it led to the founding of three vital ministries: the Wycliffe Bible Translators, the Summer Institute of Linguistics, and the Jungle Aviation and Radio Service.

Although his family did not have much money, they had a rich faith in God. At the Townsend farm in California, one book stood above all others — the Bible. Each morning Cam's father would read chapters out of the Bible to his children. Family devotions included Bible reading, a hymn, and a prayer. Cam's father always ended his prayer with, "May the knowledge of the Lord cover the earth as the waters cover the sea."

Godly character and love for those who needed the gospel were planted early inside young Townsend. It is little wonder that during his second year of college, he accepted an assignment to sell Bibles in Guatemala. Cam's missions enthusiasm was heightened when John R. Mott, a leader of the Student Volunteer Movement, spoke at his campus. He was further inspired by the life of Hudson Taylor. Taylor's pioneering spirit appealed to Townsend. If God called him to be a missionary, Cam thought, he wanted to be like Hudson Taylor.

Cam's trip to Guatemala was the beginning of a missionary career that would last more than 50 years. What he found in Guatemala troubled him. He saw that the Spanish Bibles he was trying to sell were not understood by the Indians of the rural areas. They could neither read nor speak Spanish. Cam settled among the 200,000 Cakchiquel Indians. Their confusing language had never been reduced to writing, so

Cam embarked on the task. For the next 13 years, he lived among the people, learning and writing their language. In 1929, after ten years of hard work, Cam completed the New Testament in the Cakchiquel language.

He knew he had found his life's calling. He felt that the people throughout the world who had no Bibles were asking, "Does God speak my language?" He would search them out and work to get God's Word to them. Cam soon realized that Bible translation had often been an important part of missions work. William Carey, Adoniram Judson, and Hudson Taylor were all Bible translators. But seldom had Bible translation been seen as the first job to be done.

While in Guatemala, Cam met and married Elvira Malmstrom, a first-term missionary also serving there. A valuable aide in Bible translation, she served the Lord faithfully and worked her way through the challenges of missionary life. Unfortunately, she died at a young age in 1944.

Cam's life with the Cakchiquel convinced him that missions work should focus on the unreached peoples of the world. He was deeply moved by Jesus' words of Luke 15:4: "What man of you, having a hundred sheep, if he loses one of them, does not leave the ninety-nine in the wilderness, and go after the one which is lost until he finds it?"

"Well, Lord," Cam prayed, "that settles it. Unless You definitely lead me down a different path . . . then I'm going to the one percent."

Cam finally decided to do something about his burden to train others to take the Bible to those without it. With the help of a friend, L.L. Letgers, he formed Camp Wycliffe on a farm in the Ozark Mountain village of Sulphur Springs, Arkansas. There, the small band of recruits learned

~ HEAVEN'S HEROES ~

the basic skills of linguistics, and the science of languages and how they are written. The farm property was owned by John Brown University, a few miles away. This was the beginning of a strong friendship between that Christian school and Wycliffe Bible Translators (WBT), which continues to the present. The few people in the little farmhouse probably could not conceive that they were on the ground floor of what would grow to be one of the largest independent Protestant missions organizations.

Only a year later, Cam's first Bible translators were sent to work among tribes in Mexico. In 1942, the Wycliffe Bible Translators, which received its name from John Wycliffe, the 14th-century English Bible translator, and its sister organization, the Summer Institute of Linguistics (SIL), were formed. Another helping ministry, Jungle Aviation and Radio Service (JAARS) was launched to help get the translators to their remote assignments.

Uncle Cam despised any bigotry or race prejudice and he urged non-white people to apply as Wycliffe translators. In a time when most missions agencies would not even consider it, Uncle Cam sent out two single women as a missionary team. In 1950, Wycliffe sent Loretta Anderson and Doris Cox to the headhunting Shapra tribe in Peru. The chief of the tribe, Tairi, had gained his position by murdering the former chief. But the Christian women won the hearts of the Shapras and the respect of the chief. Tairi even began helping them learn the language, and later turned away from murder and witchcraft and became a Christian. Many in the tribe followed their chief's example.

"If you had sent men," Tairi later told Uncle Cam, "we would have killed them on sight. Or if a couple, I'd have killed the man and taken the woman for myself. But what could a great chief do with two harmless girls who insisted on calling him brother?"[1]

In 1946, he married Elaine Mielke, whose work as a teacher in Chicago's schools had won her acclaim as Chicago's Outstanding Young Protestant. They were married in the home of General Cordons, former president of Mexico, and a close friend of Uncle Cam's. Uncle Cam and Elaine served 17 years in Peru where their four children were born. Then they pioneered a new work in Colombia.

After 50 years as a missionary, it would seem logical for Uncle Cam to consider retirement. However, that was not his nature. Here is what happened, as related in his biography:

> As Cam looked back on the fifty years since he'd gone to Guatemala, the old litchi tree seemed somehow symbolic of the tremendous growth of the work God had for him all along. His eyes were again on the future. "Elaine and I want to invest our next years where they will count the most."[2]

Thus, Uncle Cam found himself in the Soviet Union, studying Russian and opening discussions for Bible translation for the many languages spoken by people in the Caucasus.

Cameron Townsend not only left behind one of the largest missions organizations in the world, but he influenced many who would start similar movements. Syvelle Phillips is president of Evangel Bible Translators, a group which seeks to recruit nationals around the world in Bible translation. "I was a successful pastor in California when I met Uncle Cam," Phillips says, "but because of his encouragement, I've given my life to getting God's Word to the Bible-less peoples of the world."[3]

Through the years, Uncle Cam received many honors, often from governments in nations where SIL was helping reduce illiteracy. Offered honorary doctorates by several American universities, he declined them, fearing it would separate him from the people he wanted to serve.

Today, those involved with Wycliffe and SIL number about 5,300. Their combined efforts have produced some 578 completed translations of the New Testament. About 20 to 25 new translations are completed yearly. However, the job is far from finished — the Bible has been translated into less than half of the 6,800 languages in the world.

At the time of Cam's death in 1982, tributes poured in from all over the world. Ralph Winter, founder of the U.S. Center for World Mission, placed him with William Carey and Hudson Taylor as one of the three most outstanding missionaries of the last 200 years. Billy Graham called him "the greatest missionary of our time." But Uncle Cam himself had another opinion: "The greatest missionary is the Bible in the mother tongue. It never needs a furlough, is never considered a foreigner."[4]

LET'S BE WORLD CHRISTIANS

Why is it so important to have the Bible in one's own language?

LET'S PRAY

Pray for the approximately 3,000 groups around the world who still do not have the Bible in their language.

~ Heaven's Heroes ~

THE NAVIGATOR

DAWSON TROTMAN
(1906–1956)

LET'S REMEMBER

> *And the things that you have heard from me among many witnesses, commit these to faithful men who will be able to teach others also* (2 Tim. 2:2).

LET'S LISTEN

Dawson Trotman was one of the most creative persons of the 20th century, a pacesetter. Not only did he pioneer a certain style of ministry, but he invented new words to describe it. The term "follow-up" was probably unknown before Dawson. He made the word "Timothy" not only a proper noun but a verb to describe an older Christian training a younger one. For a sailor's spiritual food, he must take his "B rations" (Bible rations).

Trotman would be used of God to cross paths with men of vision, such as Jim Rayburn (who founded Young Life), Cameron Townsend (who started Wycliffe Bible Translators), Bill Bright (the founder of Campus Crusade for Christ), and Billy Graham. Each had separate visions, yet all were united in a drive for "world evangelization in this generation."

Dawson passionately supported the Great Commission. He believed that obedience to the mandate from Matthew 28:19–20 involved more than preaching the gospel to every creature. He was committed to making disciples, followers of Christ, from all nations.

Dawson Earl Trotman was born on March 25, 1906, in Bisbee, Arizona. A charmer, he had become the master of the double standard by the time he was in high school. As valedictorian of his graduating class, he spoke on "Morality vs. Legality," while stealing from school funds.

Dawson had little time for the half-hearted religion of his father and what he perceived to be his mother's fanatic religion. He continued to have brushes with the law. Much of this trouble stemmed from a growing abuse of alcohol. Yet his mother fervently prayed for him and urged others to join her.

A Christian neighbor called Mrs. Trotman to encourage her not to worry about Dawson: "The Lord showed me a vision of Dawson holding a Bible, speaking to a large group of people, and the burden has lifted," she said. "Don't worry about Dawson anymore."[1]

These prayers were soon answered. As a member of a Presbyterian youth group, Dawson had to memorize Scripture to gain points for his team in competition. The living Word worked in Dawson's heart. One day he memorized John 5:24: "He who hears My word and believes in Him who sent

Me has everlasting life." Dawson prayed, "Oh, God, that's wonderful — everlasting life. Oh, God, whatever this means, I want to have it. Whatever it means to receive Jesus, I'll do it right now!"[2]

Immediately, Dawson was completely committed to Jesus Christ and His cause. He formed clubs for young boys to memorize Bible verses and high school clubs that also stressed the importance of the Bible. "Immediately after my conversion," Dawson recalled, "I began learning verses, and I learned one a day for the first three years. In those years, I learned my first thousand verses."

Soon after his conversion, he met and began to date Lila Clayton, and they were married July 3, 1932. Dawson wanted further training and enrolled in the Bible Institute of Los Angeles and the Los Angeles Baptist Theological Seminary. He was a good student and especially enjoyed Charles Fuller's class on Romans.

Determined to be God's man, he challenged a friend to spend a month with him in prayer in the mountains overlooking Los Angeles at five o'clock each morning. Taking a map with them, they prayed that God would use them to minister in neighboring cities.

As their faith increased, they began to pray for a ministry across America, mentioning the states by name. Soon they found themselves praying for the privilege of preaching the gospel to the nations of the world, again mentioning nations by name. Little did they realize they were laying the spiritual groundwork for a worldwide movement. Within a decade they would see fulfillment of these prayers.

The Trotmans began to open their home to sailors who were stationed in the Los Angeles area. Out of this ministry came the first Navigators Bible study groups. Dawson trained these young sailors to share their faith in Christ.

Many Navigator men would later sail to the Pacific, and some lost their lives in battle during World War II. After the war, when the *California* was raised from the depths of Pearl Harbor, the body of a Navigator, Francis Cole, was found on his bunk with an open Bible. He was probably talking with his bunkmate about Christ at the time of the Japanese attack on December 7, 1941.

Dawson was constantly on the lookout for ways to make the Bible's truth real to those with whom he shared. In 1930, he designed a wheel representing the obedient Christian life, with balanced spokes of the Word, prayer, witness, and fellowship. Seventy years later, it is still probably the most widely used follow-up illustration.

Dawson loved the Bible, calling it "God's great love letter to humanity." And he taught the "H.W.L.W." principle — "His Word the last word." Dawson contended that our last thoughts before we go to sleep at night should be from God's Word.

The great principle of his life was what he called the "2:2 principle" from 2 Timothy. Dawson was constantly training others in the Christian life. He believed this was a great key to finishing the missionary task. He called it "reproducing reproducers." In other words, a person should share his faith with others and train them to do the same.

With every year, Dawson's fire for world evangelization grew. On an overseas trip, he saw many people engaged in religious practices with no reality of Christ in their lives. He wrote back to his young Navigators, "Kids, we've got the truth to dispel this darkness. We've got to get it out, out, OUT!"[3]

He constantly looked for better methods of sharing the gospel with others. He knew that the problem was not with the message itself. "The reason that we are not getting this gospel to the ends of the earth is not because it's not potent enough," he declared.

Dawson believed the great need was for committed young lives. "What is the need of the hour?" he asked. "It is to believe that our God controls the universe and that when He said, 'the earth shall be filled with the glory of the Lord as the waters cover the sea,' He meant it."[4]

Throughout his life, Dawson would give himself not only to the growth of the Navigators ministry, but to anyone that was involved in world missions. His life touched the ministries of Overseas Crusades, Word of Life, Campus Crusade for Christ, J. Edwin Orr's Brazil crusades, scores of Billy Graham crusades, Wycliffe Bible Translators, Young Life, Missionary Aviation Fellowship, Christian Businessmen's Committee, and Youth for Christ. He also was in close contact with Charles E. Fuller of the "Old-Fashioned Revival Hour." His close friend Erwin Moon produced the Sermons from Science films sponsored by the Moody Bible Institute.

At the East Coast Navigators Conference in 1956, Dawson drowned in a boating accident. The boat, carrying a group of skiers, suddenly wheeled in a fast right turn and then smashed against a wave. The impact threw Dawson and a young woman, Aileen Beck, overboard. Dawson held Aileen above the water until the others could rescue her. By the time the crew reached out to help Dawson, he had lost all his strength and they were too late.

When Billy Graham was informed of Dawson's death, he blurted, "Oh, God, help me to rededicate my life!"

Ever committed to doing the job well for the Lord, Dawson encouraged thousands in their walk with Christ. Perhaps *Time* magazine's tribute best describes him: "He was always holding someone up."

LET'S BE WORLD CHRISTIANS

Dawson Trotman would often challenge people to put all they knew about living the Christian life into the lives of others. Often he asked, "Where's your man? Who are you training for Christ?" Even as a young person, you can share what you know about the Christian life with another friend. Are you doing that?

LET'S PRAY

The Bible was front and center in Dawson's life. How important is God's Word to you? Let's pray that His Word will be the last word in our lives, too.

To Win for
the Lamb

Nikolaus Ludwig von Zinzendorf
(1700–1760)

LET'S REMEMBER

And looking at Jesus as He walked, he said, "Behold the Lamb of God!" (John 1:36).

LET'S LISTEN

Nikolaus Ludwig von Zinzendorf was born into a wealthy family of the Austrian nobility. His father, a high government official, died early in Nikolaus's youth. When his mother remarried, he was sent to be raised by relatives who were deeply spiritual. At the age of ten, Nikolaus sat under the preaching of the Lutheran pastor August Hermann Francke, in Halle. There, together with other young boys, Nikolaus committed himself to "love the whole human family" and to spread the gospel.

With five other boys, he formed the Order of the Grain of Mustard Seed. The six friends were bound together in prayer. Their purpose was to witness for Christ, draw Christians together in fellowship, help those who were persecuted for their faith, and spread the message of Jesus in other lands.

While still a young man, Nikolaus was one day touring an art gallery when he was captivated by a Domenico Feti painting called *Behold the Man*. It depicted Christ's suffering with the crown of thorns, and the inscription on the painting read, "All this I did for you. What are you doing for Me?"

Nikolaus was immediately struck by the question. He knew he could no longer be happy living the life of a carefree nobleman. From then on, he would seek to live only for the Savior who had died for him. Soon, he purchased an estate where, in 1722, he invited a group of refugees to form a Christian community which they called *Herrnhut*, meaning "the Lord's Watch."

In 1727, the Christian community at Herrnhut experienced a powerful awakening. The highlight was a communion service which, according to accounts of the event, signaled the coming of the Holy Spirit to the community. This ignited a fire for world missions. From this renewal a prayer meeting began which continued around the clock without interruption for more than 100 years!

Throughout his life, Nikolaus would point people past world missions to the reason for reaching out to others. He often said, "I have one passion only. It is He! It is He!" Urged by Nikolaus to "win for the Lamb those whom His blood has purchased," his Moravian followers became the most missions-minded Christian group of the 18th century. A high percentage of their membership was always serving Christ overseas. It was not uncommon for Moravians even to sell themselves into slavery, as they said, for the privilege of sharing Christ with the slaves for whom Christ died.

Nikolaus himself served as a missionary and pastor. However, his most lasting influence is as a missionary statesman. For 33 years, he was the overseer of a worldwide group of missionaries who looked to him for counsel and inspiration.

In many ways, Nikolaus was a forerunner of the great missionary movement that would follow in the next century. We remember him as a man who was the driving force behind a church consumed by their love for Jesus and, therefore, world missions. He was constantly urging the Moravians to reach into areas yet unreached with the gospel. He used his wealth and influence to motivate people in many areas of the world to open new regions to the Christian message. He said, "That land is henceforth my country which most needs the gospel."

LET'S BE WORLD CHRISTIANS

Nikolaus Ludwig von Zinzendorf used his wealth and nobility to gain influence for the gospel. What influence can you give for the message of Jesus to be spread?

LET'S PRAY

There is a great need in the Church today for young leaders. Pray that God will use your life to inspire others to live for Him and to share their wealth that others may hear of Christ.

APOSTLE TO ISLAM

SAMUEL ZWEMER
(1867–1952)

LET'S REMEMBER

> *And other sheep I have which are not of this fold; them also I must bring, and they will hear My voice; and there will be one flock and one shepherd* (John 10:16).

LET'S LISTEN

"Do not pray for easy lives," Phillips Brooks once said. "Pray to be stronger men. Do not pray for tasks equal to your powers; pray for powers equal to your tasks."

Samuel Zwemer did not have an easy life. But God granted him powers equal to his tasks.

Born near Holland, Michigan, of Dutch immigrant parents in 1867, Samuel was the 13th of 15 children. His father was a pastor in the Reformed Church. Four brothers followed their father as pastors, and a sister served 40 years as a missionary in China.

While a student at Hope College, Zwemer heard missionary-statesman Robert Wilder challenge students to reach unevangelized parts of the world with the gospel. God stirred Zwemer's heart for one of the most difficult of all mission fields, the Muslim world.

A Muslim is a believer in Islam, a religion based on the teachings of the prophet Mohammed, or Muhammad, who wrote the sacred book of their religion, the Koran. Millions of people today practice the religion of Islam, especially in North Africa, the Middle East, and southeast Asia.

Islam is an Arabic word meaning "surrender to God's will." Zwemer knew that millions of sincere Muslims wanted to know God's true will for them and that they needed to hear the good news of God's love and forgiveness through Jesus Christ. He also knew that Muslims are strong in their faith and it would be a big challenge to convert them — to do so would be "the glory of the impossible." Zwemer humbly believed that the task might be impossible for human strength but possible by the Holy Spirit.

Though denied by his church's missions board, Zwemer and another student volunteer, James Cantine, formed their own American Arabian Mission. After traveling across much of America to raise funds for the mission, Samuel Zwemer sailed for Arabia in 1890. Members of his group became some of the first Christian missionaries to Muslims in modern times. Few Christians had reached out to the Muslim world in love since the ministry of Raymond Lull in the 13th century. Most Muslims remembered only the cruelty of people calling themselves Christians who invaded the Muslims' lands in the Crusades of the Middle Ages.

Zwemer's work among the followers of Mohammed was slow and hard. But in 1895, he married a missionary nurse from England, Amy Wikes. The Zwemers continued their work among the people of the Persian Gulf, especially in the islands of Bahrain. Although they tirelessly shared the message of Jesus, there was little response. Their discouragement was coupled with grief as two daughters, ages four and seven, died within eight days of each other in 1904.

Still, they did not give up. "We must follow in His footprints," Zwemer wrote. "The pioneer missionary, in overcoming obstacles and difficulties, has the privilege not only of knowing Christ and the power of His resurrection, but also something of the fellowship of His suffering."[1]

By 1905, Zwemer's ministry to the Arab world had established four mission stations. Only a few had been won to Christ, but they were very bold and shared their faith.

In 1906, Zwemer was asked to be the chairman of the first general missionary conference on Islam that convened in Cairo, Egypt. He also helped call a second conference, held in Lucknow, India, in 1911, for those who served in Muslim lands. Zwemer was now recognized as the leading authority on ministry to Muslims. In 1912, after much prayer, he accepted a call from several missions agencies to move to Cairo and coordinate the missions activity in the entire Muslim world. He continued to speak and write in behalf of the mission to Muslims. For 40 years he edited the *Moslem World* (an English journal), and he wrote nearly 50 books and hundreds of tracts. His sleep was often interrupted by the necessity to write.

Much of his writing was directed to Muslims themselves, explaining the message of salvation through Jesus Christ. Once, an angered Muslim teacher ripped to small pieces one of Zwemer's printed booklets in front of his class. One student became curious as to what kind of powerful message would cause such anger and fear. Later, he picked up pieces of the torn booklet and put it back together. After reading the booklet, he became a Christian.

Zwemer made Cairo his headquarters for 17 years. From there he traveled the world in behalf of missions to Muslims, raising money and starting work among Muslims in India, China, Indochina, and South Africa. Although he saw few people actually turn from Islam to Christianity, his love and respect for Muslims greatly helped to pave the way for sharing Jesus with Muslims today.

In 1929, at age 62, he became the chairman of history of religion and Christian missions at Princeton University. He continued to write and speak through the rest of his life.

Zwemer's life was filled with difficulties, but he always enjoyed having fun and joking. He was even known to laugh loudly in restaurants!

Zwemer later taught at Biblical Seminary in New York and the Missionary Training Institute at Nyack, New York. At age 85, after a full life of service for Christ, this "apostle to Islam" went to be with the Lord.

Zwemer envisioned a day when many in the Islamic world would put their faith in Christ. Faithful Christian workers who had "thrown out the net" with little response would be rewarded with a great ingathering.

"By faith as we obey our Lord's commission," he said, "the time will come when Muslims will be brought to Christ in such numbers that the boats (or churches) will not be able to hold them."

Today, the Samuel Zwemer Institute continues work among Muslims. As one friend observed, Zwemer was "a man of one idea. While his interests and knowledge was wide, I never talked to him ten minutes that the conversation did not veer to Islam."[2]

LET'S BE WORLD CHRISTIANS

Samuel Zwemer worked very hard with few rewards. But what about his reward in heaven? Now that he is with the Lord, do you think he is sorry he endured hardships for Jesus?

LET'S PRAY

Ask God for the strength to keep serving Him, even in tough and discouraging situations.

ENDNOTES

Chapter 1
1. Ruth A. Tucker, *From Jerusalem to Irian Jaya* (Grand Rapids, MI: Zondervan Publishing House, 1983), p. 296.

Chapter 3
1. Sherwood Eddy, *Pathfinders of the World Missionary Crusade* (Nashville, TN: Abingdon-Cokesbury, 1945), p. 263.
2. Elisabeth Elliot, *A Chance to Die: The Life and Legacy of Amy Carmichael* (Old Tappan, NJ: Fleming H. Revell Company, 1987), p. 25–26.
3. V. Raymond Edman, *They Found the Secret* (Grand Rapids, MI: Zondervan Publishing House, 1960), p. 38.
4. Elliot, *A Chance to Die*, p. 264.
5. Ibid.

Chapter 4
1. Elisabeth Elliot, *Shadow of the Almighty: The Life and Testament of Jim Elliot* (New York, NY: Harper & Brothers Publishers, 1958), p. 247.
2. Ibid., p. 39.
3. Ibid., p. 121.
4. Ibid., p. 132.
5. Ibid., p. 236.
6. Ibid., p. 232.

Chapter 5
1. H.B. Garlock, *Before We Kill and Eat You* (Dallas, TX: Christ for the Nations, 1974), p. 44–45.

Chapter 6
1. Ibid.
2. Ibid., p. 89–90.

Chapter 7
1. Arthur Judson Brown, *The Foreign Missionary: An Incarnation of a World Movement* (New York, NY: Fleming H. Revell Publishers, 1932), p. 374.

Chapter 8

1. Eric Liddell, *The Disciplines of the Christian Life* (Nashville, TN: Abingdon Press, 1985), p. 21.
2. Katrina von Schlegel (b. 1697), "Be Still My Soul," translated by Jane L. Borthwick (1813–1897).
3. David J. Mitchell, "I Remember Eric Liddell," p. 18.

Chapter 9

1. Paul E. Little, "The God Who Never Lets Things Just Happen," *Moody Monthly* (June 1975): p. 42–44.

Chapter 10

1. W. Garden Blaikie, *The Personal Life of David Livingstone* (New York, NY: Fleming H. Revell Publishers, 1880), p. 29.

Chapter 11

1. Tucker, *From Jerusalem to Irian Jaya*, p. 234.
2. Ibid., 235–236.
3. Ibid., p. 237.
4. Ibid.

Chapter 12

1. John R. Mott, *The Evangelization of the World in This Generation* (New York, NY: Student Volunteer Movement for Foreign Missions, 1900), p. 19.
2. Ibid.

Chapter 13

1. Franklin Graham with Jeanette Lockerbie, *Bob Pierce: This One Thing I Do* (Waco, TX: Word Books Publ., 1983), p. 40.
2. Ibid., p. 41–42.
3. Ibid., p. 77.
4. Ibid., p. 149.
5. Marilee Pierce Dunker, *Man of Vision, Woman of Prayer* (Nashville, TN: Thomas Nelson Publishers, 1980), p. 252.
6. Graham with Lockerbie, *Bob Pierce*, p. 217.

Chapter 15

1. W.P. Livingstone, *Mary Slessor: The White Queen* (London: Hodder & Stoughton, Ltd., 1931), p. 21–22.
2. Ibid., p. 29.

Chapter 16

1. Lois Neely, *Fire in His Bones: The Official Biography of Oswald J. Smith* (Wheaton, IL: Tyndale House Publishers, 1982), p. 63.
2. Ibid., p. 231–232.
3. Ibid., p. 171.
4. Ibid., p. 219.
5. Ibid., p. 278.
6. Ibid., p. 296.
7. Ibid.

Chapter 18

1. Tucker, *From Jerusalem to Irian Jaya*, p. 173.
2. Hudson Taylor, *Hudson Taylor, The Autobiography* (Minneapolis, MN: Bethany House Publishers), p. 12.
3. Ibid., p. 21.
4. Edman, *They Found the Secret*, p. 18.

Chapter 19

1. James Hefley and Marti Hefley, *Uncle Cam* (Milford, MI: Mott Media, 1981), p. 67.
2. Clarence W. Hall, *Adventurers for God*, "Two Thousand Tongues" (New York, NY: Harper and Brothers, 1959), p. 119.
3. Hefley, *Uncle Cam*, p. 251.
4. Ibid., p. 182.

Chapter 20

1. Betty Lee Skinner, *Daws: The Story of Dawson Trotman* (Grand Rapids, MI: Zondervan Publishing House, 1974), p. 29.
2. Ibid., p. 30.
3. Ibid., p. 35.
4. Dawson Trotman, *The Need of the Hour* (Colorado Springs, CO: NavPress), booklet.

Chapter 22

1. Ralph D. Winter and Steven C. Hawthorne, editors, *Perspectives on the World Christian Movement*, "The Glory of the Impossible," Samuel Zwemer (Pasadena, CA: William Carey Library, 1981), p. 254.
2. Ibid., p. 253.

Marketplace Memos

by David Shibley & Jonathan Shibley
Christ-driven Power Principles
for Work and Life

› **Are you ready to make a difference?**
› **Are you tired of going through the motions and want to make what you do matter in a divinely eternal way?**

A unique collection of devotional insight and empowerment geared toward making your work and life a much more fulfilled and Christ-centered journey. Maximize your opportunities to advance the work and message of Christ through your everyday life. Don't settle for mundane when God seeks more from you and can give so much to others through your work. We have 39 powerful principles to set you on the path to a more enriching life of faith and insight.

978-0-89221-678-9 • Hardcover • $13.99

nlpg.com